from; "Doc" + Helen Watnaus

PARTING SHOTS

PARTING SHOTS

BY

DAN ISSEL

WITH
BUDDY MARTIN

CONTEMPORARY
BOOKS, INC.
CHICAGO

Library of Congress Cataloging-in-Publication Data

Issel, Dan.
  Parting shots.

  1. Issel, Dan.   2. Basketball players—United States—
Biography.   I. Martin, Buddy.   II. Title
GV884.I77A35   1985   796.32′3′0924   [B]   85-25545
ISBN 0-8092-5071-3

Published by Contemporary Books, Inc.
180 North Michigan Avenue, Chicago, Illinois 60601
Manufactured in the United States of America
Library of Congress Catalog Card Number: 85-25545
International Standard Book Number: 0-8092-5071-3

Published simultaneously in Canada by Beaverbooks, Ltd.
195 Allstate Parkway, Valleywood Business Park
Markham, Ontario L3R 4T8 Canada

To Cheri,
still the prettiest cheerleader in Kentucky,
and our children, Sheridan and Scott

CONTENTS

ACKNOWLEDGMENTS....................................ix

1   THE NIGHT I DIDN'T WANT THE BALL................1

2   THAT CRISIS SEASON: TO QUIT OR NOT TO QUIT......15

3   THINGS I NEVER COULD SAY BEFORE,
      AND PROBABLY SHOULDN'T BE SAYING NOW...........27

4   CONFESSIONS OF A SHORT, SLOW, WHITE
      CENTER WITH AN EIGHTH-GRADE HEAD FAKE........41

5   GROWING UP YEARS: BATAVIA AND BASKETBALL
      BEGINNINGS...55

6   THE MAN IN THE BROWN SUIT:
      BARON OF THE BLUEGRASS COUNTRY...................69

7   THE CAPTAIN AND THE CHEERLEADER LIVED
      HAPPILY EVER AFTER—ALMOST...................83

8   THE MAN IN THE CLOWN SUIT: DOUG MOE.........97

9   BRONCOMANIA AND THE MEDIA:
      IS THERE LIFE AFTER FOOTBALL IN DENVER?.........113

10   THE GOOSE THAT LAID THE GOLDEN EGG
      IS SICK—AND I DON'T FEEL SO GOOD MYSELF........127

11 THERE'S KAREEM, AND THEN THERE'S
THE REST OF THE KROP..................137

12 DAN ISSEL'S FIVE-STAR RATING GUIDE
AND OTHER ALL-TIME NONSENSE......................149

13 MY PAL CHOPPER AND OTHER FRIENDS
LEFT BEHIND IN THE ROCKIES..........................167

14 LOOKING BACKWARD AT LIFE FROM
DOWN ON THE KENTUCKY FARM................181

ACKNOWLEDGMENTS

When we first sat down to discuss this book, we had a simple goal: to be honest without being sensational, to emphasize the value of how hard work brings about accomplishment, and to publish a book of which we could both be proud. We feel those goals have been met, but not without help from some key people, especially our wives, Cheri Issel and Joan Martin. They not only lent great moral support, but were also instrumental in researching material, gathering photos, shipping manuscripts, and encouraging us to keep going.

We are especially thankful to Shari Lesser of Contemporary Books, who believed in this book from the beginning and provided great inspiration to its authors.

We also thank Lori-Martin Schneider for her skillful copyreading; Marcie Frankland for her rapid transcriptions of tapes; Ron Zappolo of KCNC, Denver, for his vivid recollection; *The Denver Post* library for use of its clip files; the University of Kentucky for providing background detail; and all the 1984–85 Denver Nuggets for helping an old pro go out with some style.

Dan Issel
Lexington, Kentucky

Buddy Martin
Littleton, Colorado

PARTING SHOTS

"

Did you ever walk into the ladies' room thinking it was the men's room, or vice versa? Life's embarrassing moments. And that's how I felt about that night of May 22, 1985.

"

1
THE NIGHT I DIDN'T WANT THE BALL

I shot the ball without the normal arc, almost on a straight line, but it hung in the night air of the Forum, like a hot-air balloon. It was the 23,158th and final shot of my pro basketball career. And it was taking an eternity to get there.

First, let me admit to being a shooter. There, I said it. And I feel better. Don't worry, it's not contagious, but you should wash your hands before every meal just in case.

Shooters are adrenalin junkies. Do not confuse shooters with rebounders, defensive specialists, or passers. Shooters would trade their first-born for a 50-point night. Shooters are addicted to reading their names in headlines. Shooters have themselves paged at K-Marts just to hear their names over the loudspeaker. Shooters yank the cords of Venetian blinds just to experience the sound of singing nylon mesh.

Now maybe you understand that shooters rarely pass up oportunities to pull the trigger. Which is why the situation on this night was so unusual: for one of the few times in my life, I didn't want to shoot the ball.

1

On the PGA tour, there is an expression: "Sometimes the putts just don't fall." Sometimes the basketball just doesn't fall, either. Those are the nights when you'd like to limp over to the bench, ask the trainer to put your arm in a sling, then leave the game, go outside, and move your car into a parking space for the handicapped. Anything for sympathy.

When Leonard Bernstein raises his baton expecting a B-flat from the string section and it comes out a D-sharp, that's what it's like for a shooter on a night when he can't put the ball in the cylinder. "Can't throw the ball into the ocean" is the modern cliché used by players and coaches to describe the lack of touch, which means the same thing as when they used to say: "Can't hit a bull in the ass with a bass fiddle."

The bull's posterior was not in danger on this night. I could not shoot the basketball or swing the bass fiddle. I didn't want to be in the Forum or the city of Los Angeles at that point, let alone the game. The final minutes of my 15-year pro basketball career were ticking off, and I was content to count them down from the bench, where I was avoiding the line of fire.

Meanwhile, I was witnessing the National Basketball Association's version of the Tet offensive. The Los Angeles Lakers were coming at us in waves and I was looking for either a foxhole or one of those nickel seats upstairs with Bob Uecker.

Suddenly, the coach of the Denver Nuggets, Doug Moe, was trying to convince me to go back into the game and make my last shot. Whatever possessed him to think I could get the ball anywhere near the basket is beyond me, because so far that night there was no visible evidence that my sense of geography could even get me out of the building—even with a seeing-eye dog.

That's my good friend Doug Moe, always concerned for my welfare. His Denver Nuggets were getting blown away by more than 30 points in Game 5 of the Western Conference finals. And he thought he was doing me a favor by allowing me to make a fool of myself on national TV and share in the humiliation.

Have you ever tapped somebody you thought you knew on the shoulder and discovered when they turned around it was a stranger? Did you ever walk into the ladies' rest room thinking it was the men's room, or vice versa? Did you ever say something critical about somebody to a friend and then realize the target of your attack was sitting in the booth behind you? Life's embarrassing moments. Add those all up, and that's how I felt about going back into the game that night of May 22, 1985.

I was looking for the back door, not the ball. It was all over for me now and there was no sense in prolonging the agony. I was content to leave the game as pro basketball's fourth all-time leading scorer. When you've already made more than 30,000 points in your career, what's two or three more? Especially on a night when you're one for six from the field. So when Doug stood up for the time-out and asked me to go back into the game, I started thinking of ways I could get even with him.

That's how I got down to the last shot of my career. I had planned for many years how I would face the end. My life had been in order until this moment of chaos. My horse farm in Versailles, Kentucky, a fulfillment of a lifelong dream, was ready and waiting the next day. Now in these waning moments, my coach was trying to convince me to take this Goodbye Shot so I could leave the game with one more hoop for old time's sake. As if it mattered to anybody.

To tell you the truth, I suppose it was that old fear of failure cropping up again, but not without justification. I feared that it might take me all night to make the shot; that they might stop the game, hand me the ball, ask players on both teams to step aside and say: "Here, Issel, will you please make this so we can get this game over and go home?"

That's how it's always been for me. Believe it or not, I've been scared to death of failing all my life, afraid people would make fun of the way I played. Maybe that's why I was always diving for basketballs on the floor. I figured if you tried hard, the fans would forgive you for looking so awkward. And somehow maybe this blue-collar work ethic would save you from total rejection. Now I had this one last chance at exposing my flaws. I had fooled them for 15 years, so why blow the cover in the last game of my career?

You often fantasize about your last game. You see yourself making your last shot to win the championship. You cut down the nets, hang them around your neck and then your teammates carry you off the floor, pushing Brent Musburger, Dick Stockton, and Tommy Heinsohn aside as they hand you the red phone and say: "Mr. Issel, the president is on the line from the White House." And you put the prez on hold.

Then reality sets in and you realize you're lucky if you can go out with your knees intact, a few bucks in your pocket and a chance to play for a winning team in your last season.

My reality came that night of May 22, when I realized there would be no championship. But at least it took the world champion Los Angeles Lakers to bring everything to a halt. The Denver Nuggets had enjoyed a helluva ride, winning 52 games and the division title and making it to the Western Conference finals.

Just getting this far was a remarkable feat for Denver. Doug congratulated us for making the Final Four. I felt like asking him whether he thought we'd be favored over Villanova. We certainly couldn't beat the Lakers this night, try as we did, and we were getting hammered by more than 30 points when Doug came up with this cockamamie idea of putting me back in the game.

"I want you to go back in," Doug said.

"No, Doug, I don't want to go back in. We're getting blown out. And I'm fine."

"I want you to go back in, Dan, and make your last shot. Check in at the scorer's table and let's draw up a play for you."

At the time, I probably didn't appreciate Doug's gracious gesture and I certainly didn't have a clue about the unforgettable moment that was about to unfold. My only consolation was that it was nearly 1 A.M. back east and most of my friends and family in Kentucky and Illinois had probably turned off their TVs and gone to bed. At least I hoped so.

A relative from California, Aunt Lorraine Martin, had driven more than two hours to Los Angeles just to see me play. But even she bailed out, coming by the bench in the third quarter to tell me she was going to beat the traffic. I didn't blame her. I'd have gone along with her if they would have let me.

On any other night at the Forum, most of the 17,505 Laker fans would have disappeared by then, too. Laker fans are more interested in being seen than they are in seeing. Usually they hang around long enough to make certain Jack Nicholson is in his proper place at courtside, then after being certain an important client or friend has seen them, they depart for some disco in Tinseltown, USA. But tonight they were hanging out at the Forum to watch the massacre.

I don't think it was so much the Denver Nuggets' blood they wanted to see splattered on the floor. They smelled Boston Celtic meat. It was like a reaffirmation of sorts. By being seen on TV in Boston, they were sending a message back to Beantown: "We are coming back for the title, and it is ours."

There was no way we'd beat the Lakers. After playing more than 1,200 pro basketball games, I could sort of sense these things. But I wasn't about to admit it to anyone, including the media. So I fibbed a little. "Anything is possible," I would say, resorting to a favorite expression of mine, a sort of battle cry for the Nuggets that season. I kinda believed in it, too, except that there are limits to a person's faith.

We were down 3–1 in the best-of-seven series as it shifted back to L.A. And it didn't take a genius to see that we were blindfolded, with our backs to the wall, facing a firing squad. Maybe I should have asked for a final cigarette, except I don't smoke.

Our leading scorer, Alex English, was out with a broken thumb which he had suffered in Game 4. And Calvin Natt, who was tough enough to have played Rambo in Sylvester Stallone's place, had been hobbling on a terrible knee all season. Natt's knee finally blew out in Game 4, too. He couldn't walk. I'm not sure we could have beaten our own second team in a scrimmage, let alone the Lakers.

There is a fine line between valor and insanity and we were walking it. You can play with pain but not without hope. Or without two starters. We didn't have Alex or Calvin and I came into the game with a badly bruised thigh. At the moment, however, my pride was hurting more.

Ah, the fortune of sport. Just three days ago I had been ready to climb to the top of Pike's Peak and shout to the world that the Denver Nuggets were the truth and the light. We had taken the Lakers to the max in Game 4 at McNichols Arena in Denver, only to lose out on a freak bounce of the ball. At least I thought of it as a freak bounce. Laker fans probably saw it as predictable.

Even though we lost, Game 4 will go down as one of the greatest efforts in Nugget history. We had tied the game on a pair of remarkable three-point shots in the final minutes by Mike Evans and Elston Turner. It was 116-all when the Lakers came down the court and missed five shots, getting all five rebounds, and scoring on a finger roll by James Worthy with 20 seconds left.

Talk about futility. Doug had his small lineup in the game at the time, hoping to run on the Lakers, but the big boys in the purple and gold played keep-away, like a giant volleyball team. It was like standing on your tiptoes as a kid, trying to reach the cookie jar while your big brother stood over you and kept pushing it farther and farther away from your hand.

The ball simply would not come down to a Denver Nugget, and Worthy's shot broke our backs. We lost, 120–116. Instead of being tied 2–2, with a chance to go back to L.A. and maybe steal one, we were down 3–1. We were alive, but living on a respirator.

I can still puff my chest out a little over Game 4, which may have been one of the franchise's high-water marks. It was certainly one of the most emotional games I've ever been in. When Calvin Natt hit the floor in the second half after going up for a crucial rebound, it got so quiet in McNichols Sports Arena that I thought we were filming an E. F. Hutton commercial. The fans were juiced up and they actually believed we could win. So did I. Not that I did much to contribute to the cause, but my teammates were sensational.

When I walked out of McNichols that day, I had a great sense of pride. And I certainly wasn't willing to concede upcoming Game 5, at the Forum—yet. I imagine General George Custer had better odds of winning at Little Big Horn, though, because he didn't have to face Kareem Abdul-Jabbar.

You want to know the truth? I think by Wednesday that I really unashamedly believed it was going to be my last game, no matter what I said. Okay, I admit it—I knew it would be my last game. Otherwise I wouldn't have cheated and broken Doug Moe's rule about not bringing wives or girlfriends to L.A. I'm not one to break team rules, but this was asinine. My wife Cheri had been with me since I played for coach Adolph Rupp, and for her not to be at my side now was absurd. So I sneaked her into L.A. and stashed her away at the Marriott Hotel, just a few blocks from the Hilton where the team was staying.

Some guys sleep with teddy bears for security. Me, I like having my wife around at moments like this. Although in retrospect, after the way I played and the way the Lakers blew us away, maybe Cheri could have found a more productive use of her time. After Cheri and I lunched in private, sneaking away from the team so as not to be seen, I went back to the hotel for my normal nap. Us old guys need our naps.

The average fan thinks the life of pro athletes is glamorous. If you call taking naps in the afternoon, watching soap operas and reruns of "Leave It to Beaver," and ordering room service at midnight glamorous, then I suppose we qualify. I've always slept before a game, and some people might say that I've gone to sleep in a few games, too. But this particular day, May 22, I had insomnia. So when I arrived at the Forum late that afternoon, I was still kind of groggy.

I wanted to remember this day—very likely my last as a basketball player—so I began trying to make mental notes for my scrapbook of memories. As I walked down the hallway I said to myself, "Well, this is the last time I'll ever walk down this hallway."

As I was getting taped up by my good friend Bob "Chopper" Travaglini, I said, "Well, this is the last time I'll ever get taped by Chopper."

It was probably about then I realized I was overdramatizing

things a bit. Everything was pretty much like it had been 100,000 times before, so who was I kidding? I suppose it was somewhat like the feeling you get on high school graduation day: relief. I felt pretty good about the 15 years behind me, mainly because I never thought I'd play more than five or six years. I was glad the end was coming. Quickly. And I wasn't afraid of what would happen the next day, because nothing could be worse than having to run up and down a court when your legs are wobbling and your air is gone. There was no unknown. There was no anxiety. Because I knew exactly where I'd be the next day and what I'd be doing: taking out the garbage for Cheri.

Listening to Doug Moe's pregame talks is a joy. Not that they are invigorating or interesting in the least. They're just short. I was taped and ready to go. All that was left now before running on the court for the final time was Doug's speech. I wasn't going to remember a single word, because by now my mind was on the task at hand: facing Kareem Abdul-Jabbar.

Kareem can make you look like dogmeat if you're not careful. When he launches that sky-hook over your head, he can make you feel like Fay Ray in the palm of King Kong. You just fasten your seatbelt against him and hope that he doesn't run you out of the building. Kareem is the best player in the history of basketball—has been for a long time—and if you are not totally into the game, he can embarrass you.

We were sharpening up our mental edges in the locker room, trading barbs, and getting ready for the final words of Doug. Most people would be surprised at the businesslike atmosphere of a pro basketball locker room. I don't mean we bring in our stock portfolios. We just don't holler and scream and pat each other on the back. We know what we have to do.

Which is not to say we don't laugh and joke. In the Nuggets' locker room, rapier wit often abounds. We stick the needle in each other a lot. Sarcastic humor serves two purposes: it cuts the tension and it keeps the players on their toes. You don't pull that prima-donna crap around these guys. They'll slice you up like a cheap piece of top sirloin.

I've been known to jerk my teammates around a little, but Bill Hanzlik of our squad is brutal. Hanz thinks he'll be taking my place next season—not as a player, but as the number-one needler on the Nuggets. His problem is that he never knows when to back off. He pushes Chopper to the limit.

Chop was pissed again on this occasion, as he usually was, and it was Hanzlik who got to him. I think it was something to do with his clothes. Chopper is the only guy I know who wears 17 different shades of navy blue, usually two at a time, neither of which matches anything else he has on.

It didn't take me very long to warm up, despite my old bones. It never does. I think it stems from my college days when everything was structured under Coach Rupp—do lay-ups, shoot around, and then go back to the bench for the tipoff. Some guys are early birds and like to go out on the court to shoot with players from the other team. I've always considered that treason.

If I were a fan sitting in the stands and saw players on my favorite team consorting with the enemy, laughing and jiving with each other, I'd have to wonder about how badly my team wanted to win. One minute you're shooting a friendly game of "HORSE" with a guy, and the next minute you're supposed to feel like bashing the guy's skull in? I remember a few years ago Sam Huff, the old Giant and Redskin linebacker, said it galled him to see defensive football players tackle a guy, then reach out and help him back to his feet. That's how I feel about players from opposing teams warming up together. I don't do it.

When I went out on the floor of the Forum for the introduction of the starting lineup and the national anthem, the first thing I did was look to see if Cheri was in her proper seat. When I saw her, I felt better. Actually to be honest, the first thing I did was see if Jack Nicholson was at courtside in his seat next to our bench, which he was. Then I looked for Cheri. And felt better. It kind of takes the lustre off the game if Jack's not there, because it means either he's off shooting a new film or it's not a very important game. His newest film, *Prizzi's Honor,* was completed, and since he was here, it must have been an important game.

Once the game started, everything was normal—for about three minutes. Then all hell broke loose. The Lakers were on a shooting binge. We were without our best inside rebounder, Natt, and our leading scorer, English. I felt like I was going up against Al Capone's gang with a popgun.

By the third quarter, I just wanted to make a clean getaway. I was sitting between English, who was in street clothes, and T. R. Dunn, chatting about the carnage before our eyes, when Doug called time-out. All players on the bench are required to stand during a time-out so the players from the court can sit. I stood up and that's when Doug hit me with the news about returning to the game.

He asked me what kind of shot I'd like to shoot. Before I could answer he looked up with a smile, as if a lightbulb had gone off inside his head, and said: "Shoot a three-pointer."

My shooter's instincts took over from there and I could no longer fight off Doug, so I reported back into the game. Mitch Kupchak was playing by now, and he knew that I was in the lineup for a reason. Mitch didn't want to look bad, so even though his team was winning by 30, he overplayed me. When I came around behind the pack at the three-point line, Mitch was there waiting and I didn't even get the ball. So much for Doug's great play calling.

We went up and down the court a couple more times and Mitch began to relax, playing me in a normal defensive spot. I trotted out to the top of the key and Willie White threw me the ball.

I doubt it will go down in NBA record books as the prettiest shot in playoff history, because it was a line drive. They told me later that I looked like I could barely get the ball to the basket, that it took everything left in my aging body. Assistant coach Allan Bristow said I kicked my leg while I was in the air to get a little extra oomph behind the shot.

All season long I had felt good physically except for minor nicks and dings. I approached the season 15 pounds lighter than my normal playing weight, and I was in top physical condition. If there had been a good reason, and huge stacks of money, and I had decided to postpone my retirement for another year, I felt physically capable of playing. But maybe not. Maybe I was fooling myself and all I had left was the energy for that last shot.

I'd never given a great deal of thought to the Los Angeles basketball fans, but they are generally considered fickle and not very astute. They are definitely not blue-collar, and they don't have great reputations as sports experts.

Maybe they've been given a bum rap. Because what I experienced that night left me with a totally different feeling about them: they gave me the warmest standing ovation I've ever gotten on the road in my career and one of the loudest anywhere. I guess the only one louder was the one the night they retired my jersey in Denver. Some people that night were undoubtedly applauding the fact that they were finally going to get rid of me.

The hot-air balloon finally came down, right on target. The ball had just passed through the net and hit the floor when somebody called time out. The most amazing thing about my last shot was that, even though I had no touch at all the entire night, the second I let the ball go I knew it was buried in the middle of the basket. The good Lord must have known I just didn't have much left, because His hand was guiding it right to the end. It was definitely an act of divine guidance and I wondered where He had been earlier, when I was stinking up the joint.

They stopped the game and referee Earl Strom came over to present me with a ball. I guess Earl figured he owed me that after all those lousy calls for all those years. Just kidding. Early happens to be my favorite official, and I was deeply touched by his gesture.

Kareem came over and shook my hand. People were slapping me on the back, and I almost had to look up at the scoreboard to see if by some miracle we had made up a 40-point deficit in two minutes. Nope, but all the while, the fans in the Forum were standing and cheering for me.

You're not surprised when you get a standing ovation at

home once in a while. But getting one in L.A. at a moment like this was a staggering experience. This was like James Watt standing up and applauding the Beach Boys. I was aghast and just stood there with my mouth open, drinking it in. It was a very, very special moment in my life, and I'll always have a special place in my heart for L.A. fans. As Randy Newman sings, "I Looooove L.A."

Incredibly, that horrible night was not only salvaged but turned out to be one to be treasured. There was still the matter of the score, however. We lost by 44 points and I'll always remember that, because I wear number 44. I had to explain the defeat after returning to the locker room, where reporters would be asking about my career ending, blah, blah, blah. Meanwhile Brent Musburger had sent word over via the Laker public relations man, Josh Rosenfeld, that he wanted to interview me the moment the game ended.

That caused a problem. I didn't have my three front teeth.

I've got an upper plate which I've always taken out to play basketball ever since I fell down and lost my teeth in grade school. It never bothered me that much and I plan now to have permanent teeth put in, but I wasn't too keen on going on national TV without my plate. It was bad enough that my team had gotten blown away.

You don't like to say no to Brent Musburger, however, so I dispatched a ballboy to the locker room for my teeth, which were wrapped in gauze in my shaving kit. The game ended, the ballboy wasn't back yet, and I was walking cross-court towards the CBS table, trying to figure out how I was going to break the news to Brent. Can you imagine Brent saying on TV, "Dan Issel will be here with us before a nationwide audience as soon as he can find his upper plate"?

At precisely the last second, the ballboy showed up and I was able to keep my appointment with CBS. I wasn't so fortunate, however, on matters pertaining to a parade back in Denver. The mayor, Frederico Pena, had decided to announce that afternoon that he would give the Nuggets a parade through downtown Denver the next day, even though we lost.

They forgot to tell me about it. By the time I arrived in the locker room, most of my teammates were dressed and gone. Cheri and I and our good friend Tommy Hammond, a sports announcer from Lexington, had already planned a trip back to Kentucky the next morning. We learned of the parade later the next day, which was too bad, because I would have loved to have been a part of that. Basketball teams don't get many parades in a city where the Denver Broncos are to Colorado what Mormons are to Utah—the state's biggest religion.

Eventually, the basketball that Strom had presented to me showed up in Kentucky. Chopper had my things sent to my farm in Versailles. About the third day, after the events of the week were beginning to wear off, I picked up the ball and showed it to my six-year-old son, Scott, who is a big fan.

"This is the basketball," I said to Scott in my most serious schoolteacher voice, "that Daddy played with in his last game. The one that he made the three-pointer with on his last shot."

Scott, obviously in awe, studied the ball momentarily, rolling it in his hands, then looked up and said: "You mean this basketball was touched by Magic Johnson and Kareem Abdul-Jabbar?"

All ended well, but not before some tumultuous moments that season. And just think that I almost didn't get to experience that remarkable night; I very nearly quit the team midway through the season.

"

One night after the game, when I was about to hit rock bottom, I sent for Pete Babcock, our director of player personnel. You've heard about people getting emotionally upset, crawling out on a ledge of a tall building? Well, all I did was stand there and cry, telling Pete I was going to quit. Bette Davis, in her most dramatic scenes, wasn't any more impressive—except that I wasn't acting.

"

2
THAT CRISIS SEASON
TO QUIT OR NOT TO QUIT

Three of the biggest lies in the world:
    1) The Mercedes is paid for.
    2) I've been listening to country & western music all my life.

3) Athletes never hear anything from the stands.

Of course you hear boos and catcalls and smart-ass comments. Any athlete who says he doesn't either is hearing impaired or is lying. You hear it all right. Not so much when you're playing a road game, because you become accustomed to fans questioning your heritage when you're playing in a hostile environment. But when they start booing you at home, you pick up every sound.

For some reason, a comment made by a woman from the stands at McNichols Arena in December 1984 sort of pushed me over the brink. She screamed: "Issel, you shoulda retired last year!"

That comment hit close to home. She probably had no idea that I was thinking the identical thought. Things were going terribly for me at the time and I was beginning to have some serious doubts about whether I would finish the season. I almost didn't.

One of my phobias was fear of not knowing when I wasn't good enough to play anymore. As a result, Cheri and I carefully planned retirement to avoid the embarrassment of being over the hill. Sometimes a guy can lose a step and be the last to know.

Retirement became possible on the night of July 24, 1984, when one of the horses I owned with partner Tom Gentry, an Alydar colt that would eventually be named Santiago Peak, sold for $1.6 million. I must have either been a great judge of horseflesh or a lousy negotiator of pro contracts. Because my cut on that deal was 800 grand, and I never made that in a season of playing basketball.

So the decision to quit was made right then, but the Nuggets didn't want me to announce it yet. Vince Boyrla, president of the Denver Nuggets, said I should wait until the season was over, to give myself an option. Actually, Vince wanted the leverage and *he* wanted the option of deciding if he wanted me back. So I didn't announce that the 1984–85 season would be my last. That was the beginning of trouble—big trouble—and it nearly blew up in my face.

I felt that by going public with my plans, making a declaration that I was through, I might avoid the temptation of hanging on too long. I didn't want to wind up with my 19th team in 13 years, with some coach saying to me: "We really appreciate your coming out, Dan, but we have this young kid we think can help us more in the future. You're history. So turn in your towels and don't leave any dirty jock straps in the locker."

Some of my friends fell into that trap. Mack Calvin, a great player for the Nuggets in the mid-seventies, kept hanging on beyond his time. When he announced his retirement, the Nuggets gave him a nice luncheon; members of the community, press, and team said some nice things about his career; and two months later, he was living in a Cleveland Holiday Inn, playing for the Cavaliers. Because he didn't know when it was over and what was next.

I never ended up in a Cleveland Holiday Inn, but I almost

wound up on a dusty road back to Kentucky at midnight one
December night.

I reached an emotional low in December after a pretty good
start in October and a fairly good November. I guess I was
feeling pretty sorry for myself and lonely. Cheri and the kids
had gone back to Kentucky for Christmas vacation. I had lost
my shooting touch and started hearing things from the stands
in McNichols Arena. Self-doubt was creeping up on me and I
wondered if maybe I had stayed too long at the dance. Keeping
my retirement a secret had begun to bug me, because
members of the press kept asking me "When?" and I kept
putting them off.

I was president of the Feel-Sorry-for-Dan-Issel Club. It was
getting near Christmas and we had a home game or two left.
One night just after a game, when I was about to hit rock
bottom, I sent for Pete Babcock, our director of player personnel. We went back in the equipment room, I closed the door,
and I began to bawl. Pete is a helluva guy and a great judge of
basketball talent, but it wasn't in his contract that he had to
attend to 6'9" crybabies. He stayed and listened to my tales of
woe, thank goodness, and I will be eternally grateful. He never
tried once to talk me out of quitting. He only asked that I not
quit that night.

You've heard about people getting emotionally upset, crawling out on the ledge of a tall building, and threatening to jump.
Well, I had better sense than that; besides, there weren't any
ledges in the equipment room, so I was safe. All I did was stand
there and cry, telling Pete I was going to quit. Bette Davis, in
her most dramatic scenes, wasn't any more impressive—except
that I wasn't acting. I had lost control completely and even
though I'd never quit anything in my life, at that moment I
wanted to put everything down and walk off.

I was seriously considering getting into my car that night and
driving straight through to my farm in Versailles, right outside
Lexington. And never coming back. I'd already told Chopper to
call Cheri and tell her not to go to bed, that I'd be calling her
late after the game with some news.

Thank goodness for Pete. The two of us had become good friends in a short time and I felt he was trustworthy. I couldn't go to Vince, because I already knew he didn't have my interest at heart. I couldn't go to Doug, because he would have told me how ridiculous I looked and sounded, and I'm sure he would have been right. I couldn't go to Chopper, because he would have broken down and cried with me. So I chose Pete, and it was a good choice.

To this day, I'm not sure why I was so distraught, except that it all seemed to hit me at once. Just getting all that out in a crying jag helped me feel much better. I agreed not to quit that night, but said I still wanted to maintain that option. I called Cheri to tell her my feelings and she said, "Do whatever you think is best." That relieved some pressure.

Pete joined the team on the road in a few days and we talked about it some more. Finally we agreed that I should go ahead and announce this as my last season. I left it to Pete to tell Vince and for them to figure out how we'd do it.

In January, the Nuggets gave me a luncheon, at which I retired effective immediately after the 1984–85 season. My parents were there. Vince even said some complimentary things. It was a nice luncheon and I only broke down once, right toward the end. I began to feel much better and to play better as a result. After all, we were in the hunt for the division title.

Until that point, I felt my retirement had been mishandled, especially by Vince. It wasn't the first time, or the last time, Vince mishandled something like that.

Pro athletes are less informed than the fans who watch them. We discover critical information in the damndest ways.

A fan on an airplane in Hawaii told me about the blockbuster trade that sent Kiki Vandeweghe to Portland for Calvin Natt, Fat Lever, and Wayne Cooper. I faked it and acted like I knew, because I was too embarrassed for them to find out I was in the dark. I had known something of the trade but didn't know that, as a result, I would be benched.

Professional athletes are some of the most insecure people in the world. They live in fear of being told by somebody off the street that they've been traded. I know it really set me back to have a car salesman walk up to me and ask how I was going to like coming off the bench to play power forward. I hadn't even known about the switch myself.

Cheri and I were out looking at cars that day and the Nuggets had just held a press conference about the trade with Portland. The salesman walked up and asked me how I'd like my new role. Part of the changes included Danny Schayes becoming the starting center, Cooper backing him up, and me coming off the bench to play power forward.

That was Doug's fault as much as anybody's. Handing the job to Danny Schayes on a silver platter was one of his least brilliant personnel moves, but he thought Danny might be motivated by a chance to start. Instead, Danny dropped the silver platter. He didn't go to summer camp and work as he should have. When training camp rolled around, Danny was horrible and it was becoming obvious that Cooper would be the starting center and I would back him up. Eventually Danny did come around and make some key contributions to the team later in the season, but he nearly ruined his career by being lazy.

Playing behind Coop didn't set too well with me either because, frankly, I thought I was a better center. Had I been planning to play another season and needed the statistics to bargain as a free agent, I might have screamed and argued with Doug.

That's one thing about Doug—he listens. And if you can convince him he's wrong, he'll change. He finally did let me start in the playoffs and I responded by playing better. So I made the right decision by going along with Doug's program and not raising a stink. I'll never quite get over how I heard about being benched and will always consider that a dark moment of my career. I had been a starter since eighth grade.

However, compared to what happened to Mike Evans and how Vince responded to it, my little episode was nothing.

We very nearly had mutiny on our team over the Mike Evans

incident. The club was doing well—Mike was having a spectacular year coming off the bench as a shooting guard when the newspapers got hold of the NBA salary list. Mike came to us a couple of years ago from the Continental Basketball Association, so he signed a contract at the minimum salary, about $40,000. It came out in the papers that Mike was the lowest-paid player in the NBA, which really had to hurt him.

That was bad enough, except that Vince didn't let it die there. He told a reporter from *The Denver Post* that Mike had been making a minimum contribution and "that's all he deserves to make." Why did he have to say that? All he had to do was diplomatically point out that Evans's contract was negotiated by a previous regime, and say that he was looking into it—that if Mike continued to play as well as he had, his contract would be torn up.

Instead, Vince wound up having to offer Mike a $10,000 bonus and finally to offer to renegotiate. Mike declined, saying he preferred to wait until the season ended to negotiate. I loved it.

Nothing has ever stirred up the basketball fans in Denver quite like the Vandeweghe trade. Everybody had an opinion on it, and with three talk radio shows in Denver, we got to hear most of them. Kiki was a very popular player, a scorer and a potential franchise maker.

It turned out to be a great trade, and I guess if you criticize Vince for his mistakes you also must give him credit for the things he does right. He certainly got the Nuggets back in the news. When you look at the impact it had on the team, you marvel at the outcome. We got Natt, Cooper, and Lever, plus Portland's number-two pick that year and number-one pick the next. I wouldn't be surprised if Vince didn't wind up with 100 acres of timber in the Great Northwest, too.

It worked out well for everyone, but it wasn't looking too good for Doug early in the season. And I lost my starting position. Still, it turned out to be the most rewarding season of my 15-year career since 1975, when I was a member of the Kentucky Colonels team that won the ABA championship.

Had I been forced to make a wager, however, I would have bet against Doug lasting until Thanksgiving.

First of all, at a press conference after taking over for Carl Scheer in 1984, Vince didn't exactly give Doug a ringing endorsement. He wasn't nominating Doug for Coach of the Year or throwing rose petals at his feet. In fact, Vince criticized Doug's offense—said he didn't have enough set plays—and made a point of emphasizing that the Nuggets' defense was nonexistent. The inference, of course, was that Doug didn't know how to coach defense, which wasn't true. He just didn't have any defensive players, with Kiki, Alex, and myself on the front line.

I doubt that Vince understands the passing game, even though he played for the Nicks and was a bit of a scorer himself. It is not a case of "on set play number one, you go here and on set play number two, you go there." The passing game is a reaction—acting and reacting as a unit of five individuals. And it takes a long time to learn.

You have to be able to anticipate your teammate's move. When you dribble toward a player, is he going to come and set a pick for you? Or is he going to go behind you and expect you to give him the basketball? These things must be instinctive. That's why I feared for Doug's job security. We were going to have three brand-new players in the lineup. The history of the Nuggets shows that the team struggles at the beginning of a new season after a major personnel move.

So I thought we'd get off to a terrible start and Doug would be fired before he sat down to his Turkey Day dinner. And, in a truly honest moment, Doug probably would have admitted he felt the same way.

That shows you what a poor handicapper of basketball teams I am. We had a great start, 12 wins and only two losses, and I still don't know why. It must have been because this team put winning above self more than any group of guys I've ever been around. I've played on some teams with great talent, but never on one with more desire.

There wasn't a guy on the 1984–85 Nuggets with whom I couldn't go out and enjoy having dinner. And I've never been able to say that before.

Especially if he picked up the check.

It was a great year—except for losing my job as a starter. Coming off the bench was mostly a mental block for me, because I'd started all my career. I argued with Doug that by starting me and playing me 20 minutes, I could play over a 48-minute period instead of 41 or 42 minutes and, therefore, get more rest. He didn't see it that way.

It takes a special athlete to come off the bench and make a contribution. One thing I learned was a new respect for great sixth men—Frank Ramsey, John Havlicek, Kevin McHale. There is something special about them. Me, I could never stay in the game mentally when I had to warm up, come back to the bench, and sit.

I found it very anticlimactic to go over and sit down for six or seven minutes after the national anthem. It's like the horse going on the track, warming up, and then, after putting him in the starting gate, sitting there for six minutes before springing the latch. By the time you opened the door, the horse would just fall out.

I tried like hell to make it work, to make the most out of a situation that I didn't like—playing power forward and having to come off the bench to do it. But it took away my heart. I thought I'd had a decent training camp, but I was really struggling.

Although I was a pretty good outside shooter, forward just wasn't my natural position. I think the fact that I was able to take the big centers outside with my jump shot created some problems on defense for the opponent. And I'm just not a forward.

The only other time I was asked to play the pure forward position was during the 1974–75 season with the Colonels when we won the ABA championship. Hubie Brown asked me to play it, and it was one of the worst years, statistically, of my career. Prior to that, every coach put me at center. Even when I was in the Colonel lineup with Artis Gilmore, we played a double post, high or low.

So from the time I first heard from the car salesman about

being moved to forward, I had a bitter taste in my mouth. I was shocked and hurt. To this day I'll never totally understand Doug's thinking on the matter, and I still feel we'd have done better with me as the starting center. Doug and I are still the best of friends and I'm happy the way things turned out for him, but I still want him to know I think he screwed up.

Neil Simon wrote a play called *The Goodbye Girl*, which later became a movie. As my final season wound down, I was about to become "the Goodbye Boy" in Denver. I said goodbye to every living thing in the Rocky Mountains and in most cities around the NBA. It was thoughtful of everyone, and I was flattered they cared, but after a while some of the ceremonies began to get long and boring.

One of the most memorable evenings was the American Cancer Society's "Tribute to Dan Issel," a black-tie affair which my whole family attended. There were lots of speakers, the night grew long, and my young preschool son, Scott, fell asleep on the dais. I imagine most of the people at the roast wished they could have joined him. But it was for a good cause and it wound up as a two-hour special on Denver's Channel Two, KWGN. I enjoyed it immensely, despite the length.

Some things about that night stick in my mind now. I'll never forget Carl Scheer for showing up like he did. It was tough for him to come back to Denver, to a team that fired him just a year ago as general manager of the Nuggets.

And I thought it was funny what my friend Ron Zappolo of KCNC, Channel Four, said about the number of people in attendance at the function. "Dan and I were talking," Ron said from the dais in jest, "and trying to decide how many people were here tonight. I thought it was 500 and Dan said it was 400. We asked Carl and he said he thought there were 17,500." Carl was known to pad attendance figures now and then.

One of the best lines of the night was from my teammate Fat Lever, who said, "I was finally glad I got to meet Dan Issel. When I was a boy, he was so good I thought maybe he was a black guy." And Alex English was a riot, playing the taped interviews from all my teammates on his ghetto blaster and trying to imitate Joe Cullinane, one of the local baseball announcers.

Another special evening was the night they gave me at McNichols when they retired my number. I got a bunch of nice gifts, including my own locker. Nugget owner Red McCombs, the Ford dealer in San Antonio who has since sold the team, gave me a "Kentucky blue" Ford truck which I use daily on my farm.

Some of the presentations around the league weren't as meaningful, although I did enjoy the ones in the old ABA cities. The first was Utah, where they gave me a rocking chair. Utah was always special to me because Frank Layden, one of the finest human beings in all of sports, coaches there. In San Antonio, I received some custom-made boots. In Los Angeles, my old boss Carl Scheer of the Clippers gave Cheri and me a trip to Hawaii, which was nice. The Pacers gave me a gift certificate to a Western store in Indianapolis. But at some of the places I never enjoyed going to, where they never were very nice to me, I thought it was a bit ridiculous to take up the people's time with the presentation of a plaque.

Of course, even the ones that didn't mean anything were appreciated, because it's nice to know that your absence will at least be noted.

By then, it was just a joy to me that the season was almost over and I could cherish those final days. I felt much better about everything, but I wouldn't have lasted the season in the state of mind I'd been in in December. Now that everybody knew about my retirement, I was much more relieved.

Fortunately, when it's all over, the light moments are the ones you tend to dwell on. I'm glad we had some laughs at the end, that I didn't abruptly break off my relationship with my teammates, thus never allowing me a chance to say goodbye to them, because they were special.

And even if we didn't win the championship, I was pleased I could go out on a winning team with a bunch of guys who were scratching and clawing until the very end.

My career wound up having a storybook ending. Those final days turned from a potential nightmare into a wonderful experience for my family and me. Sadly, it made it more difficult for us to leave Denver, a city we learned to love over the years.

It's over, and I have a different perspective on some things now. I'll never want to forget the special moments over those 15 years, but I don't want to relive them, either. Fortunately, I do know what's next, and it won't be a Holiday Inn in Cleveland.

Once you take off the uniform and retire, you can see some things you couldn't see before. And you can say some things you could never say before. I guess sooner or later, they were bound to come out. And this next chapter is as good a place as any to say them now.

"

I'll have to admit that, while I was aware of certain players reputations as dopers, I can't prove they were because I never saw them take it. But you can guess who they are. Look at the box scores: the dopers score 30 points one night and four the next.

"

3
THINGS I NEVER COULD SAY BEFORE
AND PROBABLY SHOULDN'T BE SAYING NOW

I love mustard. I eat mustard on my pizza. Now don't start drawing wrong inferences. I know what you are thinking—that line about Reggie Jackson when he played for the Yankees: "He's such a big hot dog, there isn't enough mustard in all of baseball to cover him." That's not the reason I love mustard, although there are some people who might think otherwise. Yes, I cared what the fans thought about me and I tried very hard to please them. But I don't think that makes me a hot dog. I never did anything in a basketball game to draw attention to myself at the expense of my team.

Okay, I admit I bitched a lot about referees. But even that had a purpose. I'm a guy who came into the game without the physical skills of a Julius Erving or a Kareem Abdul-Jabbar. I was a blue-collar player who had to scratch for everything. Sometimes I complained to officials because I was having a bad day at the office. Most of the time I just wanted the officials to earn everything they called—just like I had to earn every point, every rebound, every loose ball. Fair's fair.

If it took being hit with a technical foul to get my point across, I'd take a "T"—especially if the official was new and the call close. At least the official would have to think before he called the next one against me. That's all I wanted, an even break.

Let me say up front that I don't consider referees infallible. They blow plays just like players. It bothers me sometimes, though, that their mistakes are covered up. Coaches and players can't criticize them without getting fined. You hardly ever see an official getting a bad review in a newspaper. Why not? Everybody else in the game has to answer for their mistakes.

My least favorite officials were the ones who never missed a call. They were usually the younger ones who'd been in the league only a few seasons, and they were usually insecure about their future.

The guys who really bugged me were the ones who were above criticism. If you dared to question one call, they would punish you all night. Is that fair? Why should an official be able to dictate the flow of a game to his liking? Or slant the calls against one team, because a player or a coach said something he didn't like? Does that make for an honest game?

I have no use for officials like Joey Crawford. He's a hothead. Joey Crawford has seen too many grade D Humphrey Bogart and James Cagney gangster movies. He's always trying to be a tough guy. I don't mind tough officials, but I can't stand the ones who confuse toughness with vanity. If Joey gets mad at you, he's going to try to make you pay. Usually, after the veins pop out on his neck, you can expect the technical foul. And you'd better not talk to him the rest of the night. You can say, "Gee, Joey, don't you think we ought to talk this thing over?" And before the "gee" gets out of your mouth, he thumbs you out of the game.

So what happens is that officials wind up intimidating coaches and players. You'd be amazed how that can change the tempo of a game. A coach like Doug Moe, who always talks to the officials—it's his way of working off nervous energy during a game—is completely flustered when he runs up against a guy like Jake O'Donnell. Jake will go out of his way to make calls against a home team, just to show you that he's not afraid of being booed by the home fans. He thinks it's his duty to piss them off.

You love to see Jake show up for your road games. But once

during my final season, we were playing a critical game in Denver, making a drive for the division title. We drew Jake. Doug warned us right then not to say a word to him, no matter how bad the call might be. And Doug was the quietest I've ever seen him on the bench. Two Denver newspaper columnists from rival papers wrote that Doug had been intimidated by Jake's style. I'd have to agree with them. We won the game, but just barely. That's an example of undue influence on a coach by a referee.

Don't get the idea that I hate officials. Obviously, they are vital to the game. And I have some of my own favorites. Earl Strom is my number one. I'm not saying that Earl is necessarily the best official, but he's my favorite. For one thing, Earl has a sense of humor. He's a feisty little guy, but you can talk to him without him feeling threatened. He doesn't hold grudges and he won't let his vanity dictate the outcome of a game. In the end, when the game is on the line, Earl will swallow his whistle and let the players decide who wins and who loses—as all good refs do.

I also have great respect for Darrell Garretson and Jack Madden. They are tough officials who keep control of a game without having to intimidate. If you have a reasonable question or comment, you can approach either of them. They won't take a lot of guff, but they won't duck the hard calls either. And they won't hesitate to go against the home crowd. They are what Joey Crawford wishes he could be.

I'll also say a word about Jess Kersey and John Vanak. A veteran player appreciates guys like John, because he knows what it's like. He doesn't try to make the players look bad, and he's very fair. When he first began working, Jess let players intimidate him, but he stayed with it and developed consistency that made him into one of the most underrated officials in the league. I have a lot of respect for Jess Kersey.

Referees are such a big part of the game. Unfortunately, you can't just ignore them. I just wish there was a better system of checks and balances. They should be accountable to everyone, not just some guy back at the NBA office in New York.

New York, incidentally, was the scene of my worst experience with officials. In this case, neither Joey Crawford nor Jake O'Donnell was the culprit. Hugh Hollins and Bob Rackle were the ones involved in a very humiliating experience of mine against the Knicks at Madison Square Garden.

I got booted out of a game for a "flagrant foul" that I didn't even commit. It was the only ejection of my career and, worse yet, my four-year-old son was there to see it. How was I going to explain getting kicked out of a game?

What happened was that I went up for a rebound over the back of Paul Westphal. I had my arms out, my elbows raised. Hollins was underneath the basket with Rackle outside, and Hollins made the call. He said I committed an intentional foul. I was dumbfounded.

I talked to Hollins about it later. He said it looked to him like I was trying to throw an elbow on Westphal and he hadn't gotten any indication to the contrary from his partner, Rackle. Later on I was vindicated. I have a letter from Jack Joyce, head of NBA security, apologizing for the league and for the officials. It says that I should never have been kicked out. I was never fined.

People tell me when you are a victim of a crime, you feel powerless to do anything, that you have been wronged and there is no way to gain retribution. That's the way I felt before the anger took over. Then I wanted to punch somebody.

Someday, I'll explain the whole thing to Scott and let him read the letter.

While I truthfully can say I don't know of a single dishonest incident involving an official, I think officials are more vulnerable than players are to the wrong element. If I were a gambler and wanted to fix a game, I wouldn't go to a player; I'd go to an official. One or two calls can change the game's outcome. There have been nights when I'd like to think a referee bet on a game, but it's probably just wishful thinking on my part.

When it comes to matters like fixing games, I suppose I'm pretty naive. If you don't hear about or see something like that, you tend to think it doesn't exist. I've heard rumors, for instance, when one prominent player scored a basket at the wrong end of the court and his team failed to cover the point spread. That's a goof that can happen to a lot of people, believe it or not. But it doesn't automatically imply that the game is fixed.

No doubt I've come in contact with people who gambled on basketball over the years. I'm sure I've inadvertently given out information, not knowing whether the person I was talking to was a gambler or just some fan. But I think those cases are isolated.

Anybody who bets on pro basketball is an idiot anyway. There are so many factors that can change; it's too unpredictable. When a star player gets hurt, for instance, sometimes the team rallies around that and plays better. Look how Magic Johnson played center for the Lakers when Kareem was injured in the 1980 NBA championship game.

Then there is the inconsistency of teams' play on the road in the NBA. How are you going to set a line on a game when the Denver Nuggets play the Lakers at the Forum in Los Angeles? We beat them more than any other team in the league during the 1984–85 regular season, but then they blew us out by 44 in the last playoff game. Read the form sheet on that one and tell me what you see.

Also, how do your chart the quitters? Some players will call it a night when they're on a long road trip and their team is losing by 20 points in the third quarter. It's tough to know when those kind of guys want to play and when they don't.

There's more to what's going on than what meets the fan's eye. When a team is getting blown out by 30 or 40, sometimes it could be fatigue. When the fan sees the ball go in or not go in, he or she might not realize that the shooter could have serious, unrelated problems that are affecting his game.

When you lose a game in the NBA, it's not that critical, and you've got to learn how to bounce back from road losses. It's not like football with its 16-game schedule. We play 82 games and one isn't likely to matter that much, unless it comes down to the end of the season and you miss a playoff spot. This is where the long NBA schedule works against quality playing. Sooner or later, when a team plays 82 games, it's going to have a game in which each player is hitting on different cylinders— maybe 10 nights a year.

So anybody who bets on pro basketball is a fool who

deserves what he or she gets—or doesn't get. Give me a horse any day. At least horses don't bring their family problems to the track.

Now that I think about it, I guess the best way to fix a game, other than buying off the officials, would be to bribe a player with dope. Assuming that player took dope, he could be blackmailed into shaving points. If he doesn't shave points, you withhold his supply of cocaine or whatever. Sounds like a good plot for a cheap novel or a made-for-TV movie.

In the past few years, the NBA's image has suffered from all the stories of players being involved with drugs. Everybody knows professional athletes dabble in dope—just like truck drivers and stockbrokers and doctors and sportswriters. But, because they have so much money, so much free time, and so much stress in their jobs, athletes are more susceptible. When I hear that crap about 75 or 80 percent of the players in the NBA taking dope regularly, I think one of two things: (1) either I'm living in a Mary Poppins world or (2) I just happen to hang out with the 20 percent who don't do drugs.

Don't get me wrong. There has been—and continues to be—a serious drug problem in the NBA. I'm glad the NBA has at least recognized it, faced it, and done something about it; the worst thing would be for the league to turn its back on the problem.

I'd like to see a crackdown. For my money, the NBA is too light on second-time offenders. I'm not sure anybody should be allowed a second chance. I think a way to remedy the situation would be to say that if you're caught using drugs, you are history in the league—period. That's not very forgiving, but it would be a lot easier way to remedy it than having guys come back for two, three, four chances—which is almost making it worthwhile for a guy who has never tried drugs to feel as if he has a couple of chances coming to him.

I guess if you're going to change the rules, though, you'd have to at least allow them one opportunity to go straight. If a player was using drugs, and he didn't know the rules were going to change, he ought to be allowed one opportunity to clean up. But a player isn't going to break a bad habit like that unless he *wants* to break it.

Let me give you an example. I used to smoke up to a pack of cigarettes a day. I knew it wasn't good for me, so I quit. I missed it terribly, but I haven't smoked since then. So I've always thought that a player isn't going to break a bad habit until he decides he wants to break it (although I agree it's obviously more difficult to kick drugs than cigarettes). You can send the dopers to rehab centers all day long, but until they recognize their own problem, they'll slip right back into it.

I said when I decided to write this book that I wanted to be totally honest and candid. So I'll have to admit that while I was aware of certain players' reputations as dopers, I can't prove they were because I never saw them take it. I would be sued for libel without proof. But you can guess who some of them are. Look at the box scores for a while and watch for inconsistency in production from one night to the next. The dopers score 30 points one night and four the next. They're the guys who play four out of five games.

One big star from another city reputedly got his supply from a fireman in Denver. That was reported in the newspapers. We all pretty much knew he was a heavy doper and often marveled at his ability, considering how many years of his career he'd already blown up his nose.

I suppose the most notorious case of a player being ruined by drugs was David Thompson of the Nuggets. We all knew David was on something. Later he admitted it and got treatment, but I'm afraid it was already too late for David. As I write this, he has just been released by the Indiana Pacers and it looks like the end of his career.

David was one of the greatest kids I'd ever met when he came to the Nuggets from North Carolina State in 1976. He was happy-go-lucky, loved the game, and had unbelievable raw talent. Lordy, could this little skinny kid from the hills of Carolina sky and dunk. When he would take off on one of his dunks, you could feel the electricity as he left the floor. I was really fond of young David, so it hurt me to see what unfolded.

I'm not really sure when the wheels began to come off for

David. I think when it really hit him was after he signed the big contract for $800,000, making him the highest-salaried pro athlete in America. I doubt anybody else in the NBA, including Kareem and Doc Erving, was making even half a million then, let alone 800 grand.

The money was David's undoing, for he was unequipped to handle its consequences. A celebrity in every port, his name was David "Eight-Hundred-Thousand" Thompson. Everything you saw written about him had "Eight Hundred Grand" next to his name.

With half the NBA in an airplane at one time or another, having a basketball team pass through an airport is not unusual. Usually they don't exactly roll out the red carpet, but that year, at every place we landed, three TV cameras were rolling down the ramp to greet us—wanting, of course, to talk to David about his four-million-dollar contract.

That was the beginning of the end for David. He just withdrew, surrounding himself with shady, nondescript characters. Maybe that was the only way he could find peace. It was a tragedy, such a great talent eroding before our eyes. David Thompson was a nice person but, from then on, he would never again be that same fun-loving, outgoing kid from the hills.

Believe it or not, I've never even seen cocaine, although I've been around guys who said they took it. But I was exposed to marijuana on rare occasions, although I never smoked it myself. Maybe part of the reason I never saw it was the guys knew I wasn't a doper and kept it out of my sight.

One night on a road trip to Portland, an incident involving drugs occurred. There was no concrete proof that David Thompson was the culprit, but he certainly was a prime suspect, and he was implicated enough so that the coaches decided to take action.

Doug Moe was the coach and Donnie Walsh his assistant in February 1981. We played an afternoon game in Seattle, then waited around for the sportswriters to finish filing their stories so that they could ride on the bus with us to Portland and avoid having to rent cars or fly. We didn't leave the arena until nearly two hours after the game, and it was a three-hour bus ride to Portland, so we're talking about over five hours after the game before reaching our hotel. But on that bus trip, evidently David, or somebody, was getting desperate.

There's that old thing that you hear about when somebody takes a dump in the bathroom, burning a match will cut the smell. Well, halfway through the bus trip, David Thompson came up to Donnie Walsh and says, "Somebody just took a dump back here in the bathroom and it smells awful. Do you have any matches?" Donnie handed a book of matches to David, who disappeared to the back with Kenny Higgs, a reserve guard. About two minutes later, an aroma of marijuana wafted through the bus. I've never taken a single puff of a single joint, but I know that smell had to be marijuana and everybody else knew it, too. Including the coaches.

Some people on the bus contend that there was an 18-year-old high school kid traveling as a guest of the team who could have been the one smoking the joint. All I know is that Doug and Donnie felt David was involved and it was after that he began to play less and less. I heard later that both Donnie and Doug vowed that night they were going to get rid of him. It took a year, but they eventually did trade David. And he never did anything much as a basketball player again.

A lot of people ask me about drugs in the NBA, about the refs, about fixed games. Some also make reference to my being a minority, a white man playing a game dominated by blacks. I don't know that being white ever hurt me or helped me as a player. It certainly never bothered me that my teammates and most of my opponents had a different color skin.

It is sort of ironic that I had blacks on my high school team in Batavia, Illinois, and played against a lot of blacks in northern Illinois, but that when I got to Kentucky, the Southeastern Conference was almost lily white. It amazes me to think it was just 15 years ago that I graduated with the first black basketball player in the SEC: Perry Wallace was at Vanderbilt and his career ran concurrently with mine. If you had told people at Alabama, Mississippi, Mississippi State, and Georgia that within

15 years, they would go from calling Perry a "nigger" to supporting an all-black basketball team at their own schools, they would have lynched you.

Winning is color blind. When you are losing, some white people will say, "Well, if we had more white guys out there, it would be more fun to watch." But if players are winning, the fans would go out and watch them if they were striped.

I never really looked at pro basketball as a black man's game, but it has become dominated by blacks because they are willing to work harder to get there. Kids in the projects shoot baskets from sunup until sundown. But there aren't too many people in the projects who belong to country clubs, so you don't see many great black tennis players or golfers. It's just a matter of motivation, access to facilities, and pure numbers. As a result, the black man succeeds in this sport.

Being white and playing with and against blacks has never affected me. I'll tell you what *did* bother me, though: age.

I never got a chance to play as an average-aged center. I went right from being a young kid to an old man. One day I was a rookie with the Kentucky Colonels, a veteran ball club, with Artis Gilmore being the only other guy my age. And by the time I got to Denver, I was an old man—even though I was only 27. It all went so fast. So being old bothered me more than being a minority.

The other thing that really bothered me may seem silly to you, but it really drove me nuts: punctuality.

Yeah, I'm one of those kind of guys. I was always taught one of the rudest things you can do to a person is be inconsiderate of his or her time. I know it doesn't sound like much, but it irritates the hell out of me for one guy to hold up a whole team. That's one thing about Doug Moe that drove me bonkers: he never kept a close watch on time. With Doug, if practice was at 10 o'clock, it might start at 10:10 or 10:20. I once had a huge argument with David Thompson about being late all the time.

To me, it's like saying, "My time is more important than your time, and you have to wait on me to start practice." That's bullshit.

Some coaches won't tolerate it. Hubie Brown was one. As coach of the Colonels, Hubie had the biggest system of fines in the world. If practice was at 10 o'clock and you weren't there, taped and dressed and on the floor precisely at 10—not one second later—it was a fine. We had some guys who were terrible about it. They were late every day, and every day they paid the fine.

One year in Louisville we had $7,000 in the team's kitty for fines, and Jim Bradley was responsible for $4,500 of it. Jim was just irresponsible, and other parts of his life reflected it. When it came to running, jumping, etc., he had the greatest amount of physical talent I've ever seen. He could do things that Dr. J couldn't do. But he could never get his act together. He wandered into the wrong element, allegedly got involved with drugs, and was drummed out of pro basketball. A couple of years ago, Jim was shot to death on a street in Portland.

Perhaps his minor indiscretions eventually evolved into big ones.

Over the years, I had very few scrapes with players and management, but I had a falling out with Larry Brown in his last year of coaching the Nuggets.

Naturally, the period of depression I mentioned, in December of my last season, was a tough time, but it didn't last long and had a happy ending. I also was absolutely devastated when I was sold by the Colonels to the Baltimore Claws (no kidding, there was really a team by that name for a few days).

My longest sustained low in pro basketball and the most embarrassing time for me as a player, however, was the season of 1978–79. I was having a bad year. Maybe I was trying to find excuses for it. Larry Brown was a hyper kind of person who always was unhappy with the talent of his players. If he would have had Larry Bird, he'd have wanted Julius Erving. Or vice versa. He's the kind of guy who'd go to a restaurant, order a steak, and complain all during dinner that he should have gotten chicken because the steak was tough.

I was having a rotten season and wound up with my poorest scoring average ever—17 points. I didn't mind that David

Thompson was the main gun. I had always been the Nuggets' second main gun, and that was okay, because with the Colonels I had been second fiddle to Artis Gilmore for four seasons.

Then Larry went on one of his shopping sprees, bringing Charlie Scott and George McGinnis to the Nuggets. I felt like I wasn't even the second gun anymore—maybe I was fourth or fifth.

One night Larry came to me before a game and said: "I'm not going to start you tonight." I must have had an incredulous look on my face, I was so dumbfounded, because he looked at me for a couple of seconds and then said, "Well, never mind. You go ahead and start." The truth was, he didn't think I was good enough to start.

That's when Larry decided he wanted to dump me. He was going to trade me to New Orleans, straight up, for Rich Kelley. This stuff started getting out in the papers and I was really red-faced about it all. From the bits and pieces I've been able to learn, that's when Larry and Carl Scheer split. Larry had made all these changes, wanted to make some more, and Carl said no. It's no fun to play on a team whose coach doesn't want you. Luckily for me, Larry—and not I—was gone the next year.

Carl Scheer stuck with me, so I owe him for that. But then a lot of people in Denver owe Carl. For a number of years, Carl had to run the Nuggets on a shoestring. With bailing wire, chewing gum, and sweat, he somehow kept the franchise together, although it looked shaky in 1982 until Red McCombs bought the team and recapitalized it.

Carl is a great friend, but I know and he knows he was far from perfect. He's been criticized for some of the trades he made in Denver. Even though he only allowed coaches like Larry Brown to make the deals, as president and general manager of the Nuggets, Carl had to be ultimately responsible.

Some people say Carl got screwed when Red McCombs hired Vince Boryla as president and fired Carl. It was just a situation in which Carl had been the heart and soul of the Nuggets for so long that when Red wanted him to take a lesser position Carl couldn't do it and still maintain his dignity.

Before Carl got to Denver, basketball in the Mile High City was a joke. They couldn't fill the downtown arena with 6,000 seats.

His passion and dedication may have been Carl's undoing, because he felt the Nugget team was his baby. And it was. But he was a single parent. His child started to grow, reached maturity, and found out that there was another parent, too—Red McCombs. But Carl said, "You weren't with me during the bad times, so why should you be here in the good times?" He wanted to be singularly responsible for all of the decision making. Red, stepping forward and putting his money on the table, wanted to help raise the kid.

I've also heard that Red forced a lot of things on Carl and, as a result, Carl was sometimes afraid to make a move without consulting him. So I don't know which side of the story is correct. But I do know this: it's a shame Carl wasn't around these past two years to reap some of the benefits of his dedication.

When they write the book on pro basketball in the state of Colorado, Carl Scheer should be recognized as the godfather—if not the single parent who stayed around with the kid through puberty. It might have been Red McCombs's money that bailed out the team, but it was also Carl Scheer's heart. And remember that Red wound up making $16 million profit when he sold the Nuggets to Houston resident Sidney Shlenker in 1985. Red wound up richer. Carl wound up in Los Angeles, trying to save the Clippers. You tell me who got the best end of that deal.

None of the admissions in this chapter were that difficult to make after all. But I'll tell you one that is: the admission that I am a shooter. Or, worse yet, a short, slow, white NBA center with an eighth-grade head fake. No matter how the points went in, I always loved to score. Most players don't like to admit they enjoy seeing a large sum of points next to their names in the box score in the next day's newspaper. I admit it. Some people get hooked on chocolate; I could never get my fill of points.

"

I can remember guys hollering to their teammates, 'Don't go for Issel's head fake!' But they almost always did. After 15 years, you would think they would catch on. They didn't.

"

4
CONFESSIONS OF A SHORT, SLOW, WHITE CENTER WITH AN EIGHTH-GRADE HEAD FAKE

If all I ever had to do was shoot the basketball, they wouldn't have retired my jersey until my age surpassed the numeral on it (44). I might have played until I was 50. Unfortunately, you also have to rebound, play defense, and run the court. Shooting was my passion. The rest was work.

The thing I'll miss most about the game is the rush you experience when the shots are falling on a good night. The roar of the crowd and the smell of smoldering nets are addictive to a shooter.

Dr. James Naismith supposedly tacked a peach basket up on his barn in Springfield, Massachusetts, when he invented basketball. On nights when you get into the groove shooting, that former peach basket can look as big as a bathtub. And when a great shooter goes on a binge, it doesn't matter what defense you play against him, what shots he takes, or how many hands you've got in front of his face. When he gets that radar working, it's going in.

Although I'm not a golfer, I equate shooting to golfing. Sometimes you can hit golfballs 300 yards down the middle all day long. And sometimes they duck-hook or fade. When playing basketball, I usually could tell after the first two or three shots whether I was going to break par that night or barely be able to break 100.

Don't believe it when somebody tries to tell you all shooters are born. Maybe some are, but every good shooter I've ever seen practiced religiously. And I've seen some great ones, starting back in college with Rick Mount of Purdue and Pete Maravich of Louisiana State University, through the pros: Darrell Carrier and Louie Dampier of the Colonels, Jerry West of the Lakers, and Oscar Robertson of the Royals and the Bucks. (If you were making a film on how to shoot a basketball, you would want it to star someone like West or Robertson. Both had beautiful form, which is essential for great shooters.) And then, of course, my Denver Nugget teammates Alex English and Kiki Vandeweghe.

People may be surprised that in my list of great shooters, I'm not including Kareem Abdul-Jabbar, the all-time NBA scorer, or Larry Bird, whom many rate as the best player in the game today. Kareem isn't a pure shooter, even though he has that deft touch on his sky-hooks; he's a scorer, Bird is a shooter, a good one, as well as a scorer. Although he gets the ball in the hoop about every way imaginable, I don't think Larry stacks up with the purest shooters I've ever seen.

Shooting the basketball is fairly simple. Most of it is fundamental, but you have to program yourself until executing those fundamentals is a natural reflex. There are five or six basic steps:

1. Keep your head still and keep your eye on the target, whether it is the backboard or the rim. Do *not* look up to follow the ball in flight.
2. When you release the ball, make certain it comes off the middle and index finger last. That gives you the proper rotation, or backspin, on the ball. That gives you touch.
3. Keep your shooting elbow in and underneath the ball. Don't let it get to one side or the other, so that the ball doesn't fall off one side or the other.

4. If you keep your elbow under when you release the ball, you'll follow through. At the end of the shot, you want your elbow to be straight and your wrist broken over the top.
5. On a jump shot, you want to leave the floor and come down in the same position. You don't want to fall to either side, forward, or backward.

These are basics, but it takes a lot of practice to make them come together.

Legs also affect shooting more than people realize. That's where the fatigue factor comes into play. If you come into the game early and you're not shooting the ball well, your legs probably aren't in good shape. In fact, I'd say that legs might be the most underrated influence on shooting. Rotation and release are pretty much the same every night, but your leg muscles change. When I had a bad shooting night, most of the time it was because of tired legs.

I enjoyed shooting and scoring. Some people don't like to admit that. It's nice to be a guy like Magic Johnson, who could be a great scorer if he so desired, but chooses to put the emphasis of his game on being an all-around player. I admire Magic for being so unselfish, although sometimes he probably passes up good shots. I guess Magic invented the "triple-double" stat after all those nights he reached double figures in points, rebounds, and assists. It's great to have your own stat, although some say that that stat was actually invented for Oscar Robertson.

Me, I preferred points.

The other parts of the game besides scoring are just as important to winning, so a shooter has to set logical scoring goals for himself. He can't expect to go on shooting orgies and win games.

I always liked to get my 20 points, but equally as important was how I got them. If it takes 20 shots, of which you only make six, and eight free throws, then that's not a very good 20, you're not accomplishing much for your team. But if you take 12 shots, make six, and hit eight foul shots, then you know you've accomplished something.

The ultimate for a shooter is to go against another big gun on a night when you're both hot: a shootout. I can remember a couple of nights like that in college.

Probably the one that sticks out the most was the night I scored 53 points in Oxford, Mississippi. I was closing in on Cotton Nash's record for all-time career points at Kentucky and finally broke that after my 44th point. Coach Rupp decided to leave me in that night, and every shot seemed to be on the mark. The 53 was a single-game high at Kentucky and, considering the shooters who wore Wildcat uniforms, that was quite an honor for me.

One of the great shootouts of my collegiate career occurred my senior year when Kentucky played LSU at Baton Rouge on national TV. Pete Maravich was playing for LSU at the time and he could fill it up. In fact, he filled it up for 63. I got 51. (But *we* won the game.) That's the ultimate for a shooter—to go one-on-one with a premier player.

I still think scoring puts people in the seats. The NBA gets a lot of criticism for lack of defense, and not without justification. But look at soccer: Americans have a tough time going to a soccer match where the final score is something like 2–1. Defense wins for you, but scoring puts excitement in the game.

Lighting up the scoreboard is a shooter's delight. Besides that, there is one other experience that brings even more ecstasy: making the winning shot. That didn't happen to me frequently, but there were several occasions when it did.

When the Nuggets first joined the NBA in the 1976–77 season, the ball always went to David Thompson if the game was on the line—as it should have. David would get the ball at the top of the key and the four other players would clear out around the basket. Even when they tried to triple-team David, he would usually score anyway, sometimes drawing the foul, too. On one particular night—I'm not sure, but I think it was a playoff game against Portland—our opponents triple-teamed David, and I wound up with the ball way over in the corner. So I let it fly, mostly out of self-defense, and that shot won the game.

Maybe the luckiest shot of my career came against Utah in the playoffs my last season. We added two more free throws after the game was over, but my basket was really the game winner. It was a 20-footer that caromed off the glass and went in. I had absolutely no touch on the ball because my thumb was injured and taped. I wasn't supposed to get the ball then either. The last time I had seen the shot clock, it had three seconds on it, so all I was trying to do was throw it up and hit the rim or backboard to avoid a 24-second violation, hoping we would get the offensive rebound. Instead it went in off the glass. I take no credit—that one was pure luck. If you play long enough to shoot the ball 23,185 times, at least one of them that doesn't deserve to go in will probably do just that.

Of all the shots I've taken, the ones that used to aggravate my opponents the most were the finger rolls off a head fake—a stupid eighth-grade head fake. It worked every time. I made a living off of jerking my head back, driving around my opponent, and laying the ball in, sometimes drawing the foul and getting a three-point play. To this day, I'm as mystified by the success of that play as anyone else is.

I can remember guys hollering to their teammates, "Don't go for Issel's head fake," but they almost always did. Especially if I had just hit two or three shots from the outside on them. That was my *modus operandi*: first couple of times down the court, I'd go out to the key and hit that jump shot. After a couple of those, my man has had to come out. When he came out, I would give him the old eighth-grade head fake and drive for the hoop. After 15 years, you'd think they'd catch on. They didn't.

That's one reason I played center so much better than I played forward. I'd usually draw the other team's center in the matchups, and bigger guys weren't as mobile. For a big man to be taken outside is like a fish being taken out of water. They don't like to have jump shots in their faces all night long, and sooner or later, the fish is going to take the bait. If they don't come out, you just sit there and pop from 18 or 20 feet all night.

I've taken a few more jump shots over my career than I probably should have, although I wound up hitting 49 percent of my field-goal attempts. They always set up my drive for that stupid head fake. Hey look, when you're 6'9" and giving away four and five inches every night, you've got to come up with something innovative. Even if it is corny.

Every now and then I'd run up against a guy like Utah's Mark Eaton, whose specialty is staying home to block shots. Coach Frank Layden ordered Mark not to come out, and I loved that, because if I could stick a couple of jumpers early in the game, I was in Fat City against the Jazz and they were playing my tune. That's another reason I always loved playing against Frank Layden's teams. That and because he is one of the best coaches in the NBA.

I don't know, maybe Frankie felt sorry for me. He knows what it's like being old and fat and over the hill. Maybe he appreciated the artistry of my head fake. It probably looks like the one he used in the eighth grade in the Brooklyn schoolyards.

I'm very proud of winding up my career as the fourth leading all-time scorer in pro basketball with 27,582 points. That surprises a lot of people and makes for a great trivia question. Ask them to name the top five all-time scorers. After Kareem Abdul-Jabbar, Wilt Chamberlain, and Julius Erving, they start stammering. They might even get Elvin Hayes, number five, and then they're lost. That's when you hit them with it. "Issel?" they say. "He scored that many? Yeah, I guess he did play for a long time." I've won more free beers for people. . . .

Of course, people might argue that it's not in the record book—yet—because points scored by players in the American Basketball Association are not officially recognized by the National Basketball Association. I'm not ashamed to claim those points anyway—especially considering the great players we had in the ABA.

Eventually, the 14,659 points I scored with the Colonels and the Nuggets of the ABA will be counted. They aren't going to let Julius Erving retire without allowing his ABA points to be counted. Or Moses Malone's. Or George Gervin's. It's not as if we had no talent in the ABA: Dr. J, George McGinnis, Rick Barry, Artis Gilmore, Mel Daniels, Spencer Haywood, Connie Hawkins. . . .

Already, some of the official NBA record books are starting to include such categories as "Major League All-Time Leaders." You'll find me listed there in *The Sporting News NBA Guide.*

No one need be ashamed of the ABA.

Some of the wide-open style of the ABA rubbed off on the NBA, especially on the Nugget teams of the early eighties. We never won the championship and the closest we ever came was my final season, 1984–85. But we burned some nylon. If you liked scoring, the Denver Nuggets were the team to watch in the early eighties.

Consider these accomplishments:

- The Nuggets have led the NBA in scoring every year since 1980.
- In the 1982–83 season, Alex English and Kiki Vandeweghe became the first teammates in NBA history to finish first and second in scoring. And if I hadn't tailed off toward the end, dropping out of the top 10 to number 18, we would have been the first to have three players from the same team in the top 10.
- On December 13, 1983, the Nuggets scored 184 points in a game and lost. The Detroit Pistons beat us 186–184 in a triple overtime, the NBA's highest scoring game in history.
- Some 29 days later, the Nuggets beat the San Antonio Spurs in the highest combined regulation scoring by two teams in NBA history, 164–155.

We were never shy about putting the ball in the hoop.

Nothing beats winning. But, except for being on a contending team, it would have been difficult to have had more fun than we had on those 1982–83, 1983–84, and 1984–85 Nugget teams.

We were defenseless. They called Alex, Kiki, and me "the Big Three," but it certainly wasn't because of our shot blocking and rebounding. Kiki was the worst defensive player of the three, but Alex and I weren't far behind. I suppose I might have been the best defender of the three, which tells you how atrocious we were.

But did we have the firepower. And, believe it or not, there were plenty of shots to go around, because Doug Moe wouldn't let the guards shoot. He'd kill them if they didn't pass the ball. That's why the Nuggets were the only team in NBA history, to my knowledge, that ever had three guys average more than 20 points for more than one season.

Surprising as it sounds, members of "the Big Three" were unselfish. You don't find that often among three shooters. It seemed like whoever was the hottest that night would get the ball. This was a team where you knew that if you gave the ball up, you had a good chance of getting it back. As a result, nobody panicked or took bad shots.

That's one of the secrets to Doug's passing game: unselfish people. In Doug's system, you might get the ball two, three, four times in one sequence. You can't take an early shot; you have to be patient and move the ball. If you do that, your defender starts to relax a little, because it's human nature. And many times the ball will come right back to you, whereupon you get a better shot than you just gave up.

It was a lot of fun, a source of pride to be called "the Big Three." We knew all three of us were going to have to score a minimum 20 points each for us to have a chance of winning a game. Most nights that meant we needed a combined 70, 80, or 90 points for us to win because our defense was so horrendous.

At that point in the Nuggets' development, we certainly weren't going to be challenging the Celtics or the Lakers for the championship; it was pretty much "bombs away." But it was an entertaining style of play, and I'll admit to liking it, despite the team not always being a winner.

Alex is so remarkable. He works on that baseline like Rembrandt working on his canvas: smooth . . . supple. He rarely takes the ball to the basket. He has such long arms that he shoots the ball at the very top of his form and never has problems getting off a shot. My son Scott likes to imitate Alex, shooting as if he's in slow motion, because, to the untrained eye, Alex looks like he's shooting in slow motion.

Kiki's shooting was more similar to mine. He shot from outside and liked to take the ball to the hoop. He has an explosive first step and can beat you from the left or the right side if you let him get that step. He has great range and can bury them from the three-point line.

Maybe the Denver Nuggets won't be remembered those three seasons as having played championship-brand basketball, but hopefully some people appreciate the artistry. I did. It was a shooter's paradise.

I dearly hoped I wouldn't have to finish my career on a losing team. As glamorous as those high-scoring Nugget teams of the early eighties were, it was still unfulfilling not being on a contender.

I look back and marvel at Doug Moe's success after he took over for Donnie Walsh during the 1980–81 season. Without a lick of defense, except for defensive specialist T. R. Dunn, Doug's teams won 218 games and lost 192 during those four and a half seasons. We were in the playoffs four times. That's what makes Doug such a unique coach. He takes what material he has and makes the most of it. Give him lemons, as the saying goes, and Doug will make lemonade.

Still, at the end of the 1983–84 season, following a 38–44 record, the club had to make changes. That meant that "the Big Three" would be broken up. My career was winding down and I wasn't very valuable as trade bait. Alex was getting a little long in the tooth at 30. That left Kiki. So when Doug started shopping Kiki, he found interest in Portland. Not even Doug thought he'd get what he got for Kiki—Calvin Natt, Lafayette Lever, and Wayne Cooper.

With that trade, the Nuggets went from being a bunch of trigger-happy scorers to being a blue-collar team. More importantly, we became a complete team, for we could now play defense. Doug wanted to prove that if he had defensive players he could coach defense. And he did. During training camp, we could tell we had a good team, and Doug said so, but most of the media thought he was blowing smoke. I got excited because I knew I had a chance to go out with a winner. It became obvious we weren't going to get pushed around physically, as we had in previous seasons.

Calvin Natt probably influenced our team more than any of the other new faces. His mental toughness brought us together. I never liked Calvin before he came to the Nuggets, because he'd just as soon throw an elbow at you as look at you. He's tough. But once I got to know him, I gained the greatest admiration and respect possible. The way he kept playing with pain was an inspiration to the whole team. I think Calvin's courage, the way he went out and performed on a badly hurt knee even when he could barely walk, was the capstone of our .team.

Lafayette Lever, who is called "Fat" because one of his baby sisters couldn't pronounce "Lafayette," had his career season last year. He has two of the quickest hands I've ever seen, which is why he was among the leaders in steals and captured turnovers. Once Fat got to play more freestyle in Doug's system, as opposed to Portland coach Jack Ramsay's structured approach, his genius began to shine through.

As Fat develops his outside shot, he's going to become more of a force in the Western Conference. With Fat, T. R. Dunn, Bill Hanzlik, and Elston Turner, Denver has four of the finest defensive guards in the entire NBA. Add Mike Evans's and Willie White's shooting ability, and Denver's depth at guard is outstanding.

Of the three guys who came over from Portland, Wayne Cooper improved the most. He is a sensitive person, a nice guy, but has a tendency to get down on himself. Doug Moe wouldn't let him off the hook; when he came out of a game after a mistake, Doug would chew him out and send him back in, making him hold his head up. Coop got twice as tough mentally. His shot blocking was the first the Nuggets have had in many a season, and Coop had the best stats of his career under Doug.

When everybody talked about the trade, they forgot about

"the other trade"—the one that brought us Elston Turner from Dallas for Howard Carter. Elston quietly went about his job, specializing on defense, filling in for T. R. Dunn, and did it so remarkably well that we all forgot he should shoot. E.T.'s shooting skills were never more impressive than in the playoffs.

As for the rest of Doug Moe's team in 1984–85, role players were critical, and two of the best were Hanzlik and T. R. Dunn. Hanzlik is crazy. If Doug ever has a heart attack, it will be because of Hanzlik. Hanzlik is not a real talented player, but he knows what's expected of him. Except every now and then, just to be defiant, Hanzlik will take a shot he isn't supposed to take and Doug goes berserk. Hanzlik is the only 98-pound weakling/goon in NBA history. He will slice you up with those bony elbows, and he's a tough cookie who doesn't mind mixing it up.

T.R. is simply a player's player, a coach's player who sacrifices everything for the team. There probably aren't a lot of teams in the NBA that T.R. could play for, but Doug has a role for him: to defense the toughest guards in the league night after night and help get rebounds. T.R. plays his role better than anybody in the NBA can.

I said earlier that Mike Evans had a great year, and he did. Mike was another one of those guys who played hurt all season. He had a hurt leg and, after the incident with Nugget President Vince Boryla over low pay (see Chapter 2), hurt pride as well. But Mike could bury three-pointers with the best, and Doug usually put him in under tough circumstances, when we were down late in the game. That's pressure for a shooter. Mike is streaky, and his streaks carried us for a while. You could usually tell how far behind the Denver Nuggets were by how much Mike Evans was shooting.

Then there's Danny Schayes. Despite what you might hear, Danny's not a bad kid. He can make a contribution to the Nuggets if he's willing to work. Can he start in the NBA? Yes, I think he can one day. But to be able to reach that position, a player of limited physical ability like Danny—who is limited in things like jumping, shooting, footwork—will have to put in extra time.

I'm glad to hear Danny started going to summer camp in 1985. He didn't do that the year before, and it cost him dearly. But toward the end, when we needed to rest our centers against Abdul-Jabbar in the playoffs, Danny came in the game and played him tough—so tough, in fact, that Kareem got him in a headlock and threw him on the floor. Who knows, maybe Danny finally made his mark, right there. We called him "Sergeant Slaughter" and "Hulk Hogan" for a week after that. At least Danny knew that he had truly made a contribution to the team.

Then there are Willie White and Joe Kopicki—and you have to mention them in the same breath. When you have 11 or 12 professional basketball players on a team and only 48 minutes of playing time a game, obviously somebody has to sit. Joe and Willie sat a lot. But they sure have class.

Those spots on the team have to be filled by guys with good attitudes. They were both great. They never pouted. They were a pleasure to have as teammates. They worked as hard in practice every day as the starters did. And when a situation arose, as it did in the playoffs against Utah, when we had so many injured guards, Willie came off the bench and did his job. I thought Willie responded well. He wasn't an All-Star, but you don't expect that from a man at the end of the bench.

You might not realize it, but when a player goes in a slump, as I did in December, it helps to come to practice and see guys like Willie and Joe working their butts off, even though they aren't going to get much playing time. Just like bad ones, good attitudes are contagious.

As for Alex English, I think the way he is perceived by his teammates and coaches is much different than the way he is perceived by the press. The media see him as a recluse, a quiet guy who can score but doesn't have much personality. He's not that available to the media, and if he's got one of his charities or something to occupy his time, the press comes second—as it probably should. But somebody like myself, who always was cognizant of the media's needs and what they were saying about me, probably wouldn't put that kind of stuff on the back burner. Maybe I was too tuned in to the media, and maybe Alex has the proper perspective. Besides being a great shooter, Alex is one of the class individuals in all of pro sports. And I mean that sincerely. You always hear him saying things about Julius Erving being *the* class guy of the NBA, and he's probably right. But the truth is that Alex is not an inch behind him.

A final remark about this bunch of guys. It's a cliché to say everybody on the team was a great guy—there were no bad eggs, blah, blah, blah. The 11 guys on the 1984–85 Nuggets roster were as fine a bunch of individuals as I've ever played this game with. This even includes Hanzlik, although he's not nearly as good a gin player as he thinks he is.

As you probably can tell by now, the life of a pro basketball player is full of hills and valleys. You can flatten out those lows and highs and keep your feet on the pathway if you have a good start. I was lucky enough to have the proper upbringing in Batavia, Illinois, and down on the farm in Missouri. I hate to think where I might have wound up without the lessons my parents taught me.

"

Being tall never bothered me that much. I always got a kick out of what Wilt Chamberlain told somebody who asked him how the weather was up there: Wilt spit on him and said, 'It's raining.'

5
GROWING UP YEARS
BATAVIA AND BASKETBALL
BEGINNINGS

Sometimes you wonder how your life might have turned out had it not been for one quirk of fate. By all rights I should have played in the band or been on the debate team or done something else in place of becoming an athlete. I wasn't good at anything physical until I was in high school. But everybody needs a lucky break in life, and Wayne Nelson's leg was mine.

Wayne was a starter on the eighth-grade basketball team in Batavia, Illinois, who broke his leg halfway through the year. It was as if I had been standing down by the river, dipping my toes in the water, when suddenly somebody pushed me in and there was no turning back. Until that point, I had been a very marginal basketball player with limited skills—which is another way of saying I couldn't jump. Or run. Or shoot.

Sports had not been a major focal point of my life, mainly because I was lousy at every game I tried to play. My formative years were spent on a cow and chicken farm in Green Ridge, Missouri, near Sedalia, where my family had moved when I was four. We wouldn't move back to Batavia until I was 12, so it was on the farm that I learned about hard work. My father was trying to run a 160-acre farm, milk an entire Holstein herd, and still work eight hours a day in his paint contracting business. Dad didn't have much time for playing catch or one-on-one basketball.

So it wasn't like the movie *The Great Santini*, in which the father pushed the kid over the brink and beyond his athletic prowess. I learned that sweat was a virtue, a valuable lesson which later would become the cornerstone of my career.

Thank goodness for my family. I was brought up in a Christian home where you learned an honest day's wage was paid for an honest day's work. When I did venture into sports, I tried as hard as I possibly could. And there was no pressure on me from home to succeed. All my parents asked was that I try as hard as I could and finish the task that I started. When I see what some of the kids today have to endure from their parents, I marvel that they ever want to play sports of any kind.

At age nine I went out for the Little League baseball team and was cut. I couldn't do anything. I remember how relieved I was when I found out being "cut" didn't mean you couldn't play, only that you didn't get a uniform. You still could come and play in your T-shirt and jeans.

I have to laugh when a father comes up to me and says, "My boy is nine and throws the baseball like a girl. What can I do?" Because when I was nine, I couldn't throw the baseball as well as most girls, including my sister Kathi. That's why, when fathers ask me about their sons or daughters playing sports, I tell them three things: (1) Don't start them competing too early; (2) make sure they have fun at whatever sport they choose; and (3) don't give up on them if they aren't naturally gifted athletes.

With my two children, I hope the exposure to sports will help make it easy for them to choose. Sheridan, my teenage daughter, couldn't care less about my basketball career, which was always fine with me. She would come to the games and sit in the wives' lounge reading a book. Like me, she enjoys horses and competes as an equestrian. Scott, who is in first grade, was always too young to be aware of my career, although I think he'll remember *some* of my pro basketball years. I would like for Scott to know the joy of competition, but I don't know that I'd like him ever to be a professional athlete.

Having experienced my first failure at nine, rejection from Little League baseball, I didn't have enough sense to quit. There were many more failures to come.

That sports was not a passion for me as a young boy might have been a blessing because later in life I knew there was something else out there besides a bouncing ball. Still, that first taste of success can be intoxicating. Becoming a starter on the eighth-grade team was just that for me.

Environment can become a big influence on a young boy's athletic career. When we moved back to Batavia, a town of 7,500 about 40 miles west of Chicago, things began to change. If you didn't play sports of some kind, you were a weirdo. As you might guess, basketball was big. The entire winter social calendar was built around the high school basketball schedule.

We had an old TV set with a weak picture tube and in order to watch it in the daytime, you had to sit with a blanket over your head. My brother Greg and I would sit with our heads covered up and watch the Saturday afternoon baseball games with Dizzy Dean and Pee Wee Reese. My first sports hero was Ernie Banks of the Chicago Cubs. He was the most valuable player twice with a second-division club. And I can remember Cub announcer Jack Brickhouse yelling when Banks would hit a homer: "Hey, hey!"

Chicago's big-time sports scene was eye-popping to a farm boy in the late fifties. Occasionally we'd go to a Cub game at Wrigley Field. A young running back with the Bears, Gale Sayers, was the toast of the Monsters of the Midway. You didn't hear much about the Chicago NBA franchise. The Chicago Packers lasted one year in the NBA and were renamed the Zephyrs. In 1966, my first year at Kentucky, the Chicago Bulls joined the league.

I was in sixth grade and sort of missed the rural setting of the farm. In Missouri, I had learned to love animals, a passion of mine which later led me to the horse business, although I never had horses as a boy, only cows and calves. We had one pet calf, Sally, which my brother Greg, my sister Kathi, and I would ride around the barnyard like a horse.

By seventh grade, I was playing sports in school. I was what you'd call a late bloomer. The values I learned at home—my father's tenacity and my parents' faith—stood me in good stead, because nothing was going to come easy for Dan Issel. I was what coaches call "a project." At about 11, I became aware of sports, but it wasn't until the eighth grade I began to compete at full speed and not until my junior year in high school that I realized there was a future in it for me.

I went out for football in seventh grade but was totally ignorant of the game. They started handing out all these pads, and I had no idea where they all went. So I watched the guy next to me and mimicked him. When we got out on the field, the coach, Ken Swanson, said to us: "Boys, we're going to start out with the basics. Is there anybody here who doesn't know how many men are on a football team?" Everybody started laughing, thinking that was a pretty good joke. I went home, looked it up in the encyclopedia and discovered there were 11.

As for basketball, there was no indication that I was even going to be a good junior high school player, let alone a pro. I went out for the seventh-grade basketball team and made it, but I never got to play. I was about 5'4" but without any skills. You must understand that most kids then, as today, started playing at age six or seven, and I started in the seventh grade!

It was about then that Dad put up a basketball hoop on our garage. That was a turning point. My brother and I played in all kinds of weather, even in snow. We'd shovel the driveway and play with a glove on our left hands, so we could still dribble and shoot with the right. The following year, Wayne Nelson broke his leg, I became a starter and would always be one until my final year in pro basketball. Maybe that helps explain why I got so upset about becoming a sub in my last season.

But the struggle had only just begun. In eighth grade, I was playing more, but I was still a liability to the team, not an asset.

Most outstanding players are advanced for their age, playing on the varsity team as a freshman. I didn't even make the freshman-sophomore team as a freshman. I didn't make it, in fact, until I was a sophomore. By then I had sprouted up to 6'6". Eventually I would grow to 6'8" as a senior, then about another inch and a half after that. (Up until then I was fairly average in height. I have a picture of my junior high team when I was in seventh grade and there are four or five guys taller than me.)

I was big for my age, something all basketball players must learn to deal with. People stare at you. I've always been thankful I was a basketball player, because I'd hate for people to stare at me for being so tall and not be able to justify my height.

Being tall never really bothered me that much. You get tired of the standard "how's the weather up there" wisecracks, though, and you'd like to punch some of the wisecrackers. I always got a kick out of what Wilt Chamberlain allegedly told somebody who asked him how the weather was up there: Wilt spit on him, the story goes, and said, "It's raining."

It also annoys tall people for someone to walk up and ask: "How tall are you, anyway?" You wouldn't walk up to an overweight person and ask: "How fat are you, anyway?" People think they are amusing you when they make cracks about your size, as if it's the first time you ever heard them.

You might say I began to sink my teeth into basketball in eighth grade. Over the years, many stories have been told as to exactly how I lost my three front teeth. It became fairly obvious that I'd lost them, because I had a temporary plate which I always removed before the game. Some people speculated that I removed the plate to look mean. I did it because I could breathe better.

No, I did not lose them in a fistfight with Kenny Anderson, the Cincinnati Bengal quarterback, although I did grow up in Batavia with Kenny, who was a year behind me. I lost them while I was running. Honest.

I was horsing around in gym class. We were running laps. They had just waxed the gym floor and I was taking the curves real fast, leaning over, when I slipped and fell. When I got up, my three upper front teeth were actually imbedded in the floor. They came out, roots and all. They had to wiggle my teeth to get them out of the wood.

Imagine the horror of my parents, who had spent a small

fortune when I was a kid to make sure I had nice straight, white teeth. And I had imbedded them into the gym floor.

Having no front teeth, I guess, became one of my trade-marks. Another was my number, 44. That was something that started in Batavia, too. I had a friend, John Cory, who was very good in sports. He moved to a neighboring town, Kaneland, between seventh and eighth grade. We decided it would really be neat if we had the same number. So we picked 44. No particular reason, except that we both agreed to it. I was 44 every year from then on, except my first year with the Nuggets, because Ralph Simpson was 44. That first season they gave me 25, the number of Dave Robisch, who they had traded for me. Ralph was traded the next year and I got old number 44 back.

Life in Batavia was fairly simple. We swam at the old rock quarry, a huge swimming pool and meeting place for kids. We played sports. And for excitement there were the bright lights of Chicago.

In high school, sports became increasingly important to me. I was always trying to keep up with my friend, Dean Anderson, the best basketball player in our class and the most athletic boy, but he always seemed to stay ahead of me. When I was on the freshman team, he made the frosh-soph squad. The frosh-sophs got to play the preliminary game before the varsity team on Friday nights. The freshmen played on Monday afternoons. When I made frosh-soph, he was on the varsity as a sophomore. Dean could really shoot, but what I admired most about him was that he was better than me and more advanced as a player. I was always chasing Dean, who was also the starting quarter-back on our football team.

Finally, at the end of my sophomore year, I began to close ground. I'll never forget the night of a tournament in Kaneland when I first dunked the ball. I made a steal at half court and caught the team going the other way. It probably surprised me more than anybody, but I took it and dunked it. Suddenly, I was blossoming. Prior to that time, nobody ever expected me to be above average.

I quit football after my junior year because I was starting to get letters from colleges about my basketball future. I also went out for the cross-country team just to build up my legs and wind but only practiced and never competed. Basketball was going to be my game.

Probably the best thing that ever happened to Dan Issel's basketball career was that Batavia hired a new coach between my sophomore and junior year. Don Vandersnick was a tough guy, a marine drill sergeant type who believed in discipline. If Coach Vandersnick said that jumping in the Fox River would make you a better basketball player, by noon the next day half the parents in Batavia would have their kids down at the bridge, ready to dive off.

I think Coach Vandersnick's favorite pro football team must have been the Green Bay Packers, because he certainly seemed enamored with Vince Lombardi's coaching methods. We would go in a half hour before school started, slip off our street shoes, put on gym shoes, and shoot free throws and jump shots. Then, after practice, we would work another two hours. Plus he would keep me another 45 minutes after practice.

That's what it was going to take, though, for me to become more than just another high school player. As a junior, Dean and I were starters with three seniors—Jerry Sytar, Larry Heidleberg, and Tom Skea.

The good times were about to begin.

Like all boys, we were curious. One day Dean, Tom Skea, and I decided to go to Chicago. After about a half hour of looking at cars at the Auto Show, we split and started to cruise the streets. We were walking down South State Street when a black guy approached us and said, "You guys want some girls?"

Although we were all thinking the same thing, Dean was the only one crazy enough to say yes. He said his name was Slim and that we would have to drive him to a place to find these girls, so we began to walk down the street toward my car. While we were walking, Slim kept ducking in and out of alleys, talking to his friends. When we got to the car, Slim and Dean got in the back, Tom and I in the front. Just as I was about to pull the car out, I looked up and saw a guy in front of me with a gun pointed right at us.

Luckily, it was a cop.

The cop told us that Slim was a con artist who was going to take us into an alley and roll us for our money. At first, Dean tried to fabricate a story and cover for Slim, but the cop threatened to take us downtown and lock *us* up. We began to spill our guts. They took Slim downtown instead.

We got in the car, drove away, and never looked back.

That's about as exciting as life ever got for boys in Batavia. Except when the state basketball tournament rolled around— which was another kind of excitement altogether.

The state of Illinois had more than 700 high schools in those days, and the competition for the basketball championship was open to all classifications. The smaller schools would usually get eliminated in the district. From there it was on to the regional, then a sectional, a super-sectional, and the state tournament. Both my junior and senior year, Batavia was the last small school eliminated from the district. The town went crazy.

The *Chicago Tribune* wrote stories about our team and our town. My junior year we had an excellent team and we lost in the finals of the district. That's when I got my first form letter from a college and it opened up a whole new world. All five of us starters would eventually get college scholarships. In my senior season, Dean was back, we had Mike Brown at one guard, and Kenny Anderson at the other. By now, we were starting to get noticed—and recruited.

Dean went on to North Texas State, played for a year, dropped out, and came back home to Batavia. The last time I heard, he was in the printing business.

My uncle Floyd Meyer was always a loyal supporter of mine, even when I played for the Nuggets. The first two years I was in Denver, Uncle Floyd drove up from Colorado Springs, more than 75 miles, just to see our games. But nothing he ever did in Denver could match his performance in Batavia. You've heard of the "hat trick" in hockey? Uncle Floyd pulled the incredible "coat trick."

We were playing in the sectionals my junior year and I got a couple of questionable calls against me early. Next thing you know I had a third foul in the first quarter and had to sit on the bench. Uncle Floyd was livid. As the referee was running down the court, Floyd threw his overcoat at him. It was a perfect ringer, right on the ref's head. They stopped the game and gave the coat to the superintendent. My father wasn't very happy about being the guy who had to go and retrieve it.

At long last, it began to look as though the Issel project might be successful. I was apparently good enough to play college basketball, because the offers began pouring in during my senior year. My father decided that he and coach Vandersnick would screen them. That was fine with me but it looked like a foregone conclusion that I was going to Northwestern, because that's where my parents wanted me to go.

The pressures were awesome. For a 17-year-old kid to have all kinds of people visiting his little hometown and asking him to play basketball, it was heady stuff. Dad and Coach Vandersnick decided we wouldn't talk to anybody until the season was over. We had college scouts coming to our house at all hours of the day and night, trying all kinds of scams, all of which my father could see through. We'd have scouts from the West Coast calling us at 11 P.M. Scouts would come to the house to talk at night and my dad would fall asleep on them. For example, Bruce Hale from Miami came up to see us with this beautiful hour-long recruiting film. It had the girls on the beach, Rick Barry shooting in the gym—the whole nine yards. And when he turned on the lights after it was over, my dad was sitting in his chair, snoring.

My dad lost his patience only once—with a recruiter from the University of Illinois. Illinois never was in the picture anyway, but Bill Small had been captain of and a great player for the Illini, and he hailed from Aurora, one town down from us on the river. He came to my house with Howie Braun, then the assistant coach at Illinois. We sat down at the dining table to talk, even though they knew I wasn't interested. Howie took out an envelope and put it on the table and he proceeded to tell us not how good Illinois was, but how bad Northwestern and Wisconsin both were. And that, being from the state of Illinois, I owed it to the school to go there.

When he got through with his spiel, my dad said: "Well, Mr. Braun, that's very nice, but we're not interested in your school." The first thing Braun did was pick up the envelope. Then he went off on a temper tantrum, like he had lost his head. My dad had to grab him by the forearm and shoulder and usher him to the door; he threw him out of the house, with Bill Small trotting along behind apologizing for Howie's behavior.

It was the only time we were blatantly offered cash—although we never opened the envelope, so we can't say for sure. My dad and I regret to this day that he didn't open the envelope just to see what was inside it before he threw Howie Braun out of the house.

We decided to cut it down to four schools. Visitation was unlimited back then and I could have visited more than 100 if I'd so desired, but four was enough.

So far, the only recruiting trip I had made was to Wisconsin, which had joined Northwestern as a leading candidate. There was some interest in Iowa, but instead of going there, we went to see the Hawkeyes play a game in Chicago Stadium. Michigan played a game there, too. They invited me in and I remember going to see Cazzie Russell. He was an incredible player, but what I remember most about Cazzie was that he wore boxer-shorts underwear with a drawstring in them. Man, that was hot. Being a boy from Batavia where everybody wore boxer shorts, I was amazed that this great basketball player wore shorts with a drawstring. See what impresses a young high school kid?

Kentucky was yet to come.

Batavia was a wonderful place to grow up and I enjoyed it immensely, but the place I would eventually live was in the Bluegrass Country. That's funny, because I love my parents, my brother, and my sister. To this day, my dad and brother live two doors apart in Batavia. We see a lot of them, since we're only about seven hours apart by car. And we are still very close.

How close our family is was demonstrated a couple of years ago, when my brother Greg became ill and needed a kidney transplant. The kidney must come from a close family member, and I was a candidate to become Greg's donor. That would have meant the end of my basketball career, of course, but at that point I'd had a very long and happy career, so giving Greg a kidney was certainly more important than playing basketball. That prospect did not bother me at all.

I was not compatible, however, and my father was. The hero of this story, my dad, stepped up to the plate, so to speak, and gave Greg one of his kidneys in November 1982. It worried me, for I had read that what the donor has to go through is much worse than what the recipient has to endure.

But it has been a very successful operation. My father is a painting contractor and Greg works for him. They both work 40 hours a week now. Sometimes, when people talk about heroes in sports, I have to laugh.

If there is a lesson to be learned from the story of my upbringing, other than the importance of a good, solid family life, it is that there is hope for kids who aren't blessed with ability at an early age. Our society might have a tendency to go at it a little early, to have the kids competing too soon.

I was allowed to make my mistakes, to learn by trial and error. How often today can athletes say that? By being allowed to fail, I became more aware of how imminent failure could be. And so I worked harder to avoid it. I remember in high school, my English teacher told me if I didn't put my head into the books that first year in college that I'd be back home in Batavia after the first year. My first semester I made a 3.75, the highest grade-point average of my college career. I was scared of failing.

The kid who couldn't make the Little League team at nine, who couldn't throw a baseball as well as a girl, who couldn't make the frosh-soph team as a freshman—that kid was going to be a college basketball player.

So don't give up on those kids when they are 13 or 14. You have to encourage them, make sure they are having fun at what they are attempting. Don't push them so hard that they give up on sports. It's a delicate balance, but you have to minimize the competitiveness with the maximum of enjoyment.

If your son or daughter strikes out in the bottom of the ninth with the bases loaded, he or she wants to minimize it, to enforce the idea that "it's only a game and it's not that important." It isn't life or death. Kidney transplants are.

I will never forget my first recruiting letter. It was from the University of Wisconsin. One of those stupid forms where they ask you for your height, weight, honors, etc., then you sign it and mail it back. Before it was over, I would have 150 of them. But Wisconsin's was the first. I opened it and read it over and over again. I guess that's when it first hit me I was going to be something more than an average high school player.

My parents had still been pushing for Northwestern. But John Erickson was coaching at Wisconsin then, and he came to my high school graduation. I'll always remember the graduation present he gave me—Bill Bradley's book, *A Sense of Where You Are*. I was trying to find out where I was and where I was going myself.

All my friends were putting down Northwestern. They were telling me it was a rich kids' school, a "floozey-doozey school," where the girls wore mink stoles to fraternity parties. I was reared to believe you did what your parents told you to do, and so I figured Northwestern was where I'd probably end up. So I visited the campus with a guy named Ron Koslicki—I think that was his name—who was a basketball player there. He took me to a big variety show that McLean Stevenson, Debbie Reynolds, and other famous alums usually attended.

After the show, Ron and his girl took me to a hamburger joint. What freaked me out is that Ron Koslicki ate his hamburger on a bun with a knife and fork. All my friends' remarks about it being a rich kids' school set off bells in my head. Because Ron Koslicki ate hamburgers with a knife and fork, I didn't go to Northwestern.

So I signed a letter of intent with Wisconsin. But my parents weren't happy with that decision, because they thought it was a big party school.

Meanwhile, I had made a visit to Kentucky. But when I got on campus, I picked up a student paper and read an article on recruiting. It listed the two top Kentucky choices at center: George Janke of St. Rita High in Illinois and Joe Bergman, who was supposed to be the best in the country. I turned the page looking for my name, but it wasn't there, and I was crushed. They listed 15 players, but not Dan Issel. I figured that, even though Lexington was a nice place, they didn't want me. So I went home.

What I didn't know was that Janke had signed with Dayton and Bergman went somewhere in Iowa. And that suddenly Kentucky's interest in Dan Issel was about to heat up again.

So one night my dad came to my bedroom and said, out of the blue, "You know, if you really want to be a college basketball player, there's no better place you could go than Kentucky."

I almost fell out of my bed. That was the first time either he or my mother had said anything about any school except Northwestern. I think I was so relieved that I could go someplace besides Northwestern and still please them that I would have taken Slippery Rock. Besides, I loved the country in Lexington and was captivated by the horse farms and Keeneland on the drive from Bluegrass Parkway to the campus.

We went back for a second visit to Kentucky, even though my father had to pay for it. The plane landed at Bluegrass Field and we had to walk downstairs to reach the terminal. As we pulled up, they brought out the stairs and unrolled a long red carpet. Everyone started looking around the plane to find out who this celebrity treatment was for.

It was for my father and me. As we stepped off the plane, a sign at the top of the terminal read: "Welcome to Lexington, Home of the Kentucky Wildcats."

Joe B. Hall, Harry Lancaster, and Coach Rupp all met me at the airport this time. I didn't know much then about the legendary Adolph Rupp, who was getting on in years and near the end of his career. But I was soon to learn a great deal about "the Man in the Brown Suit."

"

It didn't look good for a school with the basketball heritage of Kentucky not to have a single black player. And it didn't take our opponents long to start exploiting the race issue. To hear some of them tell it, we were playing under white hoods and Coach Rupp was the Imperial Wizard of the Ku Klux Klan.

"

6
THE MAN IN THE BROWN SUIT
BARON OF THE BLUEGRASS COUNTRY

Down South in 1967, two men loomed larger than life. Both of them were college coaches in the Southeastern Conference, one football, one basketball. Any boy growing up within earshot of the Deep South know all about Bear Bryant of Alabama and Adolph Rupp of Kentucky—except me. I didn't know much about Kentucky's legendary basketball coach, except that he was legendary. I might as well have come to Lexington from Batavia on a truckload of pumpkins— instead of taking an airplane for the first time in my life. Coach Rupp didn't make recruiting trips anymore, so I had come to the mountain.

And I was trembling with fear. It was like having an audience with the Pope. Joe B. Hall, then the assistant coach at Kentucky, had prepped me by saying, "He [Coach Rupp] will say something that you will think is hysterical, but if he doesn't laugh, don't you laugh. Then he'll say something that you think is pretty dumb, but if he laughs afterward, you laugh too."

Coach Rupp was a tough, grizzled old man. He talked tough, looked tough, acted tough. Yet he had mellowed somewhat by then because hc had come to a crossroads in his life. Tough as he was, Coach Rupp wasn't the tyrant he was alleged to be back in the post-World War II days. People were starting to whisper that the game of college basketball had passed him by. There were no blacks yet playing for the Wildcats, and just the year before, the all-black University of Texas at El Paso team had beaten Coach Rupp's all-white team in the NCAA finals. The dynasty was imperiled.

It wasn't until the next trip back to Lexington that Kentucky offered me a scholarship. I signed on to try and help preserve the dynasty.

You have to understand the state of college basketball in the mid-sixties. John Wooden's UCLA dynasty was in its infancy. With a youngster named Lew Alcindor at center, the Bruins were on their way to seven straight NCAA titles, nine out of ten years and ten out of twelve. UTEP had come from out of nowhere to win the NCAA tournament—the only championship any team besides UCLA that would win for a decade. In other words, Kentucky's salad-day years were waning while UCLA's were waxing.

Not that coach Rupp needed to apologize for his record. Nobody coached more college basketball victories than the Baron—825 wins and only 190 losses. His Kentucky teams couldn't match the incredible UCLA streak, but neither could anyone else's teams. Under Rupp, Kentucky had won four NCAA titles and 23 Southeastern Conference titles and were SEC co-champs twice. The last NCAA championship, however, had come in 1958, nearly two decades before.

As Bob Dylan sang in 1964, times they were a-changin'.

Which is not to say that Coach Rupp wasn't still running the show at Kentucky. There was no foolishness or horsing around. In fact, looking back on it now, I think Coach Rupp and his assistants hoped that by being tougher on the players they would make up the talent deficit that existed due to the absence of blacks.

As a freshman, I was exposed to Harry Lancaster's bootcamp tactics. Harry was both the freshman coach and a varsity assistant. He was flat-top all the way, right out of the recruiting brochure from Parris Island. I'll never forget the day he lowered the boom on Bill Busey.

Busey was a little guard from Shelby County, Kentucky, one of those gym rat types who always has a basketball in his hand—and, of course, is always dribbling it. He had a bad habit of dribbling while Coach Lancaster was talking to the team. I had never heard anybody speak harshly to a player before (boy, was I going to be surprised when I met Doug Moe) but Harry lowered the boom on Bill Busey the second day of practice: "Busey," he said, "if you dribble that ball one more time while I'm talking, I'm gonna nail your ass in a coffin and ship it back to Shelby County."

That kind of stuff will get your attention. Bill stopped dribbling.

The seeds of revolution were not yet planted on the Kentucky campus. Antiwar sentiment and rebellion were still several years down the road, and Kentucky was fairly right wing. But the athletes were beginning to change, starting to question authority and resenting Rupp and Lancaster's demanding physical regimen. It helped me, because I had become accustomed to the hard-nosed approach to coaching in high school.

The situation at Kentucky my first year was great for me, because our varsity team was awful when I was a freshman. The worst team in coach Rupp's career finished 13–13. The program was suffering a hangover after the loss to UTEP. Coach Rupp had a small team in 1966—"Rupp's Runts," they were called—but the Wildcats were heavily favored to beat UTEP. Some people say that Rupp never recovered emotionally from that 1966 upset.

The freshman team, full of Great White Hopes, went 18–2 my first year. With Coach Rupp's health beginning to deteriorate, Harry Lancaster began to do more and more coaching of the varsity. Eventually, Harry would become the athletic director, Coach Rupp's boss.

Kentucky was still trying to win with white boys only, an effort that would prove futile, and pressure on Kentucky to recruit a black player was mounting almost daily. One story making the rounds, part of which was probably apocryphal, had to do with Wes Unseld, a black player who went on to become a great center with the Baltimore/Washington Bullets. Kentucky had supposedly tried to recruit Wes the year before, but was unsuccessful when Unseld received some nasty letters, postmarked from Lexington, telling him to stay away. Coach Rupp's critics liked to claim that about half the letters were in his handwriting.

I don't know whether or not calling Coach Rupp a racist would be accurate or not. If he was prejudiced, I don't think it was intentional, although some of my black friends say that unintentional racism is the worst kind. Let's say that, like most people in Lexington at that time, if he was a racist, he was ignorant of it.

Coach Rupp would have terrible memory lapses, especially with names. I don't know why, but he never forgot a player's hometown, even though he sometimes couldn't remember the player's name. Bob McCowan of Dayton, Ohio, was never "Bob." To Coach Rupp, he was "Dayton." It's a good thing he never signed Jeff Ruland of the Bullets, who was from Lake Ronkonkoma, New York.

Some people will say that Coach Rupp gave me favored treatment. I've heard and read that he's said that, if he were starting a team, he'd want to build it around Dan Issel. That's very flattering, of course, and I'm not sure why he'd choose me, with all the great players Kentucky has had. Probably because I came along at a time when his program was about to falter and in an age when athletes were beginning to question authority. I was from the old school. In the sixties, when campuses would soon be aflame with rebellion, Coach Rupp was probably just thrilled to have a player who wouldn't challenge him.

As a sophomore, I played center on the varsity, and Coach Rupp stuck with me, even though I was struggling and he had a senior center, Cliff Berger, on the bench. He could have gone to Cliff at any time, because I was scoring in the single digits and wasn't much of a factor in games. We started three sophomores—me, Mike Casey, and Mike Pratt—so it took a while for us to come on. I remember one game, against Georgia, I was knocked out the second half, didn't score a point, and spent the night in the medical center.

At this point, people were beginning to write off our team. Coach Rupp and Ray Mears of Tennessee had a terrible hatred of each other. We went to Knoxville and they blew us out by 28, the worst defeat ever for a Rupp team. The Wildcats were looking like pussy cats and there were serious doubts about the program. But Coach Rupp stayed with us and we repaid him by beating Tennessee in Lexington, 60–59, and clinching the SEC title on the last game of the regular season by beating Vanderbilt, 85–80.

We had stopped the bleeding—for a while.

It didn't take our opponents long to start exploiting the race issue. To hear some of them tell it, we were playing under white hoods and Coach Rupp was the Imperial Wizard of the Ku Klux Klan. Admittedly, it didn't look very good for a school with the basketball heritage of Kentucky not to have a single black player. So that would soon change.

The first guy to jump on the race issue was Al McGuire. He did it two straight years, the first time at the end of my sophomore year. We were playing against McGuire's Marquette team in the Mideast regional tournament which was held, of all places, in Lexington. Just 16 teams played in the four regionals and everybody said the Kentucky-Marquette game would decide which team would represent the Mideast at the Final Four.

By then, I was playing better, usually hitting my 20 points a night. In the regional, I had to go up against this black guy, "Helicopter" Hentz. They didn't nickname him Helicopter because he stayed in one place. So McGuire shot off his mouth, telling everyone, "Issel has been playing against these white stiffs. He won't get 20 points against this kid, because Helicopter can jump out of the gym." There I was at the opening tap, a portly white kid who can't jump a lick, face to face with

"Helicopter." I got the opening tap. It was as if I were pumped up with a bicycle pump: I got 36 points and we beat McGuire, and Helicopter, rather handily, 108–96.

Kentucky basketball was back. We aimed our sights at the Final Four. Only one problem: somebody forgot to tell Ohio State. They beat us on a last-ditch bucket, and they went to the Final Four.

About the so-called deal Coach Rupp made with me on the school scoring record of 2,138 career points: it's true; we did make a deal.

Joe B. Hall became assistant varsity coach and head freshman coach in the fall of 1969, and decided that our team needed a beefed-up running program. So we ran. And ran. And ran. On Monday, Wednesday, and Friday, we ran sprints. On Tuesday and Thursday we ran distance. We ran up to five miles, then worked out with weights. We gradually increased the number and the distance of our sprints until we were doing twelve 220-yard and 20-yard dashes a day. And they all had to be under 30 seconds. That might not sound like much but, believe me, we had guys hanging on the fence, begging not to have to run anymore.

When he first came back to Kentucky in 1965 as a recruiter, Joe B. had convinced Coach Rupp that running would help the program. Nobody hated the running worse than Louie Dampier, who didn't like Joe B. The feeling was mutual: Joe B. had called him a "prima donna" after Dampier's 1966 All-American season. So Louie tried to defy the spirit of the workout without refusing to do it. He was a master at getting his foot on the finish line just as the stopwatch struck 30. Joe B. would be counting ". . . twenty-eight, twenty-nine," and just as Joe B. would say "thirty," Louie's foot would hit the finish line. Every time.

By fall of '69, athletes were starting to speak out on such matters as Vietnam all over America. We hadn't advanced that far yet at Kentucky, but some of our players were ready to rebel over Joe B. Hall's running program.

So the players called a meeting.

Kentucky was still getting the cream of the crop of white players, but attrition was beginning to have an impact on the program. The year before I arrived, they had signed five kids. Three of them flunked out and one transferred. Phil Argento was the only player left in the class ahead of me. So in my class they had signed a dozen players, including: Mike Casey, the "Mr. Basketball of Kentucky"; Mike Pratt, the best player from Ohio; Randy Pool, the best player from Tennessee; and Travis Butler, the best player from Alabama. With those four, we had nine high school All-Americans, including me, Jim Dinwiddie, Terry Mills, Clint Wheeler, and Benny Spears. Kentucky could get whatever players it wanted (except, apparently, Wes Unseld).

The demanding physical regimen took its toll on the team, running off some very talented players during my four years there. My roommate my junior year was Greg Sterrick of Illinois. He transferred to the University of Southern Illinois as a sophomore because he couldn't take the kind of treatment Kentucky was dishing out. I think as a high school player, Greg had led the nation in free-throw shooting. Another kid, Mark Soderberg from Huntington Beach, California, was the heir apparent to my job as center. But he wound up leaving, too, for the same reason. Randy Noll from Northern Kentucky left and went to Marshall. It's hard to say how good they would have been if they'd stayed, but it was the team's loss when they left.

So maybe the fact that we were having a team meeting to discuss the rigors of Joe B.'s running program was a good idea after all. It was better than having more people quit. The players decided to boycott the running program and instigators Randy Pool and Art Laib sent me in as spokesman to inform Coach Rupp.

"First of all," I said to Coach Rupp, "I want you to know that this wasn't my idea. But some of the guys think the running program is a little tough and they don't want to do it."

"How do you feel?" Coach Rupp asked me.

"I don't really know if it would be fair for me to tell you how I feel about it," I said, trying to remain objective.

"Well let me ask you this, " he said. "Have you looked at Cotton Nash's all-time scoring record at the University of

Kentucky"—he never said "UK," he always said "University of Kentucky"—and thought about the possibility of being the player who could break it?"

This was Rupp at his best, knowing exactly how to motivate a player by dangling a carrot. And it was always the right carrot. He knew I was a shooter and a scorer.

"Yes sir, I have," I said. "And I have thought that was a good possibility."

"Good, then you go out and run today and I'll do everything within my power to see that you obtain that record."

I went out and ran.

Five freshmen went with me. I don't know what transpired after that, but I know the following day everybody was back out at the track.

The funny part about it is that if he hadn't bribed me with Cotton's record, I was ready to cash in my chips, because I was damn tired of the running program, too. That was the genius of Rupp. And he stuck to his word: there were nights when he left me in the game an extra 3 or 4 minutes so I could get my 34-point average. But the stories I've heard about him leaving me in with four scrubs just so I could catch Cotton are not true.

He never did like Cotton Nash, because Cotton was his own man. He had been the all-time leading Kentucky scorer in average (24.6), followed closely by Cliff Hagan (24), who was one of Coach Rupp's favorites. Cotton was also, at that time, tops in career points for three-year players (1,770). I passed him on the same night I established the individual-game scoring record of 53 against Old Miss. As I was walking off the court, Coach Rupp said, "Well, I'm kind of sorry you broke Cliff Hagan's record. But I sure am glad you broke that son-of-a-bitch Nash's record."

That was a beginning of a special relationship that I enjoyed with Coach Rupp, although he would never let on that he'd done anything for me. Later, I developed a close kinship with the Baron. I owe everything that I have accomplished in basketball to him. I doubt that if I had gone to another school I would have been durable enough to last 15 years in the pros.

Rupp was very superstitious. If he found a hairpin before he went into an arena, he believed that meant good luck. Our trainer, Claude Vaughan, would get off the bus and drop several hairpins in Coach Rupp's path, so that he'd be certain to find one. He was even superstitious about his wardrobe, which is how he got the nickname of "the Man in the Brown Suit." When he coached high school basketball in Rockford, Illinois, he owned one suit, a brown one he wore until it got ratty. When he'd saved enough money, he bought a new suit—a blue one. The first time he wore it to a game, his team got blown out and he never wore anything but brown after that.

Coach Rupp could be mean, but not mean-spirited. It's just that he was very disciplined. Most coaches kick you in the butt one minute and pat you on the back the next; Rupp just kicked you in the butt all the time. Maybe that's because his style of play required a disciplinarian approach to timing, technique, and coordination. Also, he was a disciple of the fast break, which he brought with him from Kansas as a player under Phog Allen.

There were certain things Coach Rupp frowned upon. One of them was married players. I'll never forget the day I went to see him, in between my junior and senior years, to tell him I was getting married to the head cheerleader, Cheri Hughes. It was a bit of a charade, which went like this:

"Do you have to?" he asked me.

"No," I said.

"Well, there has only been one player get married that didn't have to since Billy Ray Lickert in 1958," he said.

I wasn't going to be deterred. "Well, I'm getting married, Coach," I said.

"When you're married, basketball is no longer number one," he frowned.

"Coach, with this girl," I said, "basketball hasn't been number one for a long time anyway."

He grunted. "Well, I can't tell you not to get married," he said. "But I don't like it."

Then, for a wedding present, he and Mrs. Rupp sent a beautiful silver tea and coffee set, probably the nicest wedding present we got.

Another charade was having to ask for tickets. I'd ask for extra ones, because my folks would be driving down from Batavia and Cheri's folks would come to the game. In the three varsity years I played there, my folks missed just three games, and they would usually bring my brother or sister and another couple, so I always needed tickets. The scenario was the same every time I went to see Coach Rupp:

"Coach, I need two tickets for Saturday night."

"Damn, son, do you realize how much I could sell those tickets for?"

"Yes sir, I realize they are hard to get."

"Well, I don't think I'm going to have any extra. But if I do, I'll give them to you on Saturday."

On Saturday there were always two extra tickets in the top of my locker. He just wanted you to know that he was the boss and you were lucky just to be playing at the University of Kentucky. In many ways, he was right.

My last two years at Kentucky were outstanding. We won the SEC championship both times, but we never got out of the regionals. At the end of my junior year, our good friend Al McGuire came back for revenge. We started Casey, Pratt, Phil Argento, Larry Steele (who went on to play for Portland), and me—all of us white.

One of our managers, Doug Billips, going over to Marquette's locker room for tape before the regional game, heard McGuire bringing up the racial stuff again. Doug came back and told us what McGuire said to his players: "When you go out there and warm up, you look down at Kentucky's end. You won't see any niggers down there on their end. They don't like niggers in Kentucky. They don't think niggers should be playing on their basketball team."

Well, McGuire's tactics worked. We were favored to win that regional again, but they beat us with a team that included George Thompson, who later became an excellent NBA player. The race issue was starting to haunt Kentucky basketball, although by that time Kentucky was recruiting Tom Payne, an excellent black high school player who eventually broke the color barrier at UK.

Still, we had a helluva team coming back for my senior year. Coach Rupp was 68. Joe B. was heavily involved in the coaching, but we had resolved many of the differences over the running, etc.

We had everybody but Argento back that year. We'd won the SEC and it looked as if we were going to be great guns. Mike Casey and I had traded turns as leading scorer—he was it my sophomore year, I was it my junior year. Mike's style of play was not unlike Larry Bird's: he didn't have a lot of natural ability, but he had an innate sense about where the basketball was going to be and could see everything on the court.

Except that Mike was in a car accident that summer. He hit a telephone pole, broke his leg, and didn't play. Even without him, we had an outstanding year. We lost one game (to Vanderbilt), and since UCLA had lost to Southern Cal, we went into the tournament as number one in the polls.

Jacksonville had two 7-footers, Artis Gilmore and Pembrook Burrows III. But the guy who did the most damage to me was a tiny point guard named Vaughn Wedeking. I had 28 points but was in foul trouble. While I was running down the court, he stepped in front of me and drew a charge for my fifth foul with more than 10 minutes to play. Then our whole first team wound up fouling out and we lost, 106–100.

If we had gotten some scoring out of our guards, and if I hadn't screwed up by getting into foul trouble, I think we might have beaten Jacksonville that year and gone to the Final Four. And to this day I believe that, if Mike Casey hadn't had that car accident, we would have won the NCAA title. But, of course, there was still UCLA. Sidney Wicks ate Artis's lunch and the Bruins won the title again.

Two years after I graduated and went on to play for the Kentucky Colonels, Coach Rupp retired. He didn't want to retire, but he was 70. Some of us even tried to get the Kentucky law changed so he could coach past 70. I did a TV commercial on his behalf, but that just offended Joe B., who thought I was trying to deprive him of his rightful coaching turn at UK. I thought Joe B. would have admired the player's loyalty to his former coach, but that wasn't the case at all. Joe B. must have remained bitter, because in all the years he coached there, he never once asked me to help him recruit. Even when I was playing for the Nuggets and he signed two Denver kids, he never even asked me to visit them on Kentucky's behalf.

Coach Rupp went to work for the Colonels, not as a coach, but on the board of directors. A few years later, Mike Pratt and I ran some basketball camps together with Coach Rupp and we became close with him. After the Colonel games, sometimes he would come over to the house. Coach Rupp liked to have a bourbon or two, but in later years, the doctors had told him to cut back. One night when he was visiting us, I made a bourbon and took it to him. He declined, much to my surprise.

"The doctor told me to lay off the hard stuff," he said. "You got any vodka?"

When he retired in 1972 and they took the basketball away from him, that was the beginning of the end. I was sad when he died. But I will never forget the Man in the Brown Suit. He was truly the Baron of the Bluegrass.

I doubt anybody will ever fill the shoes of Adolph Rupp at the University of Kentucky; they were too big. That was one of the problems that Joe B. encountered. Even when Joe B.'s Kentucky team finally won another NCAA title in 1978, people didn't warm to him. And when Joe B. retired in Denver after the Western regional in 1985, there were no tears.

The Kentucky basketball job is a plum. It carries an estimated salary, including perks, of up to $1 million a year. So, when Joe B. retired, there were a lot of applicants. One of them wasn't me.

A rumor got started that I was a candidate because my name was on some official list. No chance. It was never close. I'm sure I was never really considered, but I did get a call from the Kentucky athletic director, Cliff Hagan. It was something like: "You wouldn't like to have your name submitted to the coaching selection committee, would you?" I thanked Cliff and told him no. He said, "I have several calls like this to make. I also have to call [Laker coach] Pat Riley to see if he's interested."

They say you should never say "never," so I won't. Somebody

might call tomorrow and make me an offer I can't refuse. But I can't imagine what that would be. I've worked very hard for 15 years to be able to sit here on this farm, to do the things I love doing, to be with my family and not have to put them second. In coaching, I'd have to get back into all the traveling again.

And then there is the credibility factor. It's important for me to leave sports with a good name. It wouldn't take me very long as coach of Kentucky's basketball team to tarnish that name. Just a losing season or two. I look at Craig Morton, the former Dallas Cowboy and Denver Bronco quarterback. I think Craig was as popular an athlete as ever played in the city of Denver, and I thought he lowered himself a couple of rungs when he took the job coaching the Denver Gold of the United States Football League. And then getting fired was devastating. That's one thing I hope to avoid.

A quick commercial on the University of Kentucky: I think it's the best place in the country to go to school, for one who is serious about basketball. Kentucky is at the very top of the list, which includes UCLA, North Carolina, Notre Dame, etc. The treatment you receive from people all over the state of Kentucky is overwhelming.

In addition, Lexington is a great place to be. I could take you right now into downtown Lexington and walk into the offices of 10 former basketball players who grew up outside the state of Kentucky but came back to make their home here because they love it so much. Cotton Nash, Tom Parker, Scotty Baesler—on and on and on. There are so many great opportunities there, both in basketball and after basketball.

That's why, when I got the chance to play pro basketball and stay in Kentucky, I jumped at it. The captain of the Kentucky Wildcats, now married to the head cheerleader, signed on with the Kentucky Colonels. We moved up the road to live happily ever after.

Almost.

❝

You know how they always run weather warnings across the bottom of the TV screen? Well, Cheri and I were watching TV one night when we saw a strip that read: 'Dan Issel has been traded to the Baltimore Claws. Details at eleven.'

❞

7

THE CAPTAIN AND THE CHEERLEADER LIVED HAPPILY EVER AFTER—ALMOST

When things start going well, that's the time to worry. Life after graduation from Kentucky was nothing but one big chocolate nut sundae with whipped cream and cherries on top. I was a kid in an ice-cream store, lapping up every moment.

In 1970, I was happy as a fat pig in the sunshine, living out a storybook fantasy. I'd married the prettiest cheerleader on the Kentucky squad, and I had some jingle in my pockets. Instead of waiting for the NBA draft, I accepted an offer from the ABA because they were putting a franchise in Louisville, just up the road from where Cheri grew up. The captain was keeping the cheerleader at home.

The Kentucky Colonels seemed as indigenous to Louisville as swallows to Capistrano. Basketball and horse racing belong in Kentucky as soccer belongs in Europe.

The Colonels had some wealthy and influential owners, along with some dynamic young businessmen: John Y. Brown, owner and founder of Kentucky Fried Chicken and soon-to-become governor of the state; Wendell Cherry and David Jones, the founders of Humana, an extended health care organization and the place where the first artificial heart implant was done;

David Grissholm, who now runs Citizens Fidelity Bank, one of the largest in the state; and Stewart Jay, a successful Louisville attorney.

So this was no fly-by-night franchise, and John Y. would turn out to be a fairly good nocturnal aviator. But my flight was going to get bumpy.

Life in Louisville was an extension of college, except better. For the first time ever, I wasn't broke. They paid me to play hoops and I didn't have to attend class anymore. I averaged, more than 29 points a game and shared Rookie of the Year honors with Charlie Scott of Virginia my first season. The Colonels won the division title the next year, when I averaged more than 30. And achieved the ultimate in 1975, winning the ABA championship.

What else could life have to offer? Well, for one, growing up in a hurry. I was about to learn that pro basketball was a business, not a game.

It is about the time that a man gets knocked on his butt that he realizes the value of being married to a good woman. Luckily, I had the best. But she didn't come easy.

Cheri and I met after the season started my sophomore year. My roommate, Mike Casey, and I spotted Cheri, a pretty little blonde, at about the same time, and we had a bet about who would take her out first.

However, Cheri was from Lexington and going steady with a local boy. "Practically engaged" a friend of mine told me. So neither of us two jocks could get this cheerleader to go out for a soft drink. We asked her out all season, but we both kept striking out.

Our season was almost over when we clinched no worse than a tie for the SEC title in Athens by beating the Georgia Bulldogs, 106–87. These were joyous times for Kentucky fans because we had pulled our esteem out of the ashes. We cut down the nets, took down the goal, and were celebrating up a storm. Then, just before we got ready to fly home to Lexington,

Cheri surprised me by consenting to ride home with me from the airport. I was ecstatic. For the first time in three months, I finally got my toe in the door without getting the door slammed in my face. I felt like I had scaled Pike's Peak.

The players flew back in a different plane from the cheerleaders. When we got to Bluegrass Field, more than a thousand people were there to greet us, and one of them was a girl I had been dating. Afraid her presence would ruin my evening with Cheri, I got rid of "the other woman" somehow—I think it was my eighth-grade head fake. I gave Cheri a ride home that night—she lived with her parents, Mary and Virgil Hughes— and our romance began to blossom. As she was getting out of the car, I asked her what she was doing tomorrow night.

"Going to the library," she said.

"What about Saturday?" I asked.

"I already have a date," she said.

"Well, I'll call you," I said. True to his basketball upbringing, old Issel would not quit without a fight.

The next night Cheri called me and asked if I would like to see a movie. To my knowledge neither of us has ever gone out with anybody since then. So I guess I won the bet with Casey. More importantly, I won the hand of a woman who I love dearly. But our Camelot story was about to hit some rough patches.

Some people might say that I made a huge mistake signing with the ABA. I don't think so, although I do agree that I was stupid not to wait until I was drafted by the NBA. (Eventually, after I had signed with the ABA, the Detroit Pistons took me in the eighth round). I had been a consensus All-American and no doubt would have been among the top five draft picks—which would have given me a great deal of leverage with the ABA. But money has never been my prime motivation. I've always put other things first, such as the city where I live and the people I work for.

The Dallas Roadrunners of the ABA, later to become the Dallas Chapparals, had drafted me. The ABA came after me immediately following the Wildcats' loss to Jacksonville, wanting me to sign that weekend. I told them the only way I would be interested was if Louisville had a franchise.

Mysteriously, two days later Louisville had a franchise and owned my draft rights.

We had begun negotiating with the ABA before the NBA draft, which wasn't exactly brilliant. But the Atlanta Hawks had the number-one pick and we'd talked to the Hawk front office a good bit and got a feel for what the money would be, and it wasn't that different from what the ABA was offering. So, with Cheri being from Lexington and me being in love with Kentucky, I went ahead and signed a five-year contract with the ABA.

It was for less than a half-million dollars over the five years.

The ball club made it sound much bigger, and newspapers said it was closer to $1.4 million. (When you read about a guy like Steve Young of the Los Angeles Express USFL team getting a multimillion-dollar contract, you can bet that it's considerably less.) I had some annuities, some insurance, and a $50,000 signing bonus.

That was still a huge sum of money for a farm boy. Cheri and I had been living in a one-bedroom apartment close to the Kentucky campus. The only furniture we had was a king-sized bed that my folks gave us for a wedding present and what stuff we had confiscated from the basement of Cheri's parents. As soon as I signed, we bought a two-story, three-bedroom, already furnished, Tudor model home in Louisville. It was like suddenly being released from welfare.

When everything is going great and all the universe appears in order, there is no reason to think that tomorrow can bring heartache. The Easter bunny and Santa Claus were still real to me. The Colonels had won the 1975 ABA title in five games against Indiana with a starting five of Artis, Louie Dampier, Will Jones, Bert Averitt, and me.

And we had a great summer. Artis and I went on an ABA-NBA trip to Japan with our wives. While I was overseas, I got a phone call from my attorney and friend of many years, J. Bruce Miller. (As I've said before, I always seem to get the damnedest news in the damnedest places.) Bruce told me he had gotten a call from John Y. Brown and that he might have to trade me. Since I had a no-trade clause, I wasn't too concerned.

John was then the sole owner of the team. Two years before, it was almost sold to a couple of brothers in Cincinnati. But the word began to leak out and it got into the newspapers, and the story was that one morning John Y.'s little boy came to the breakfast table crying, "Daddy, is it true that the Kentucky Colonels are going to be sold to Cincinnati? It's not, is it?" John Y. told him it was true, and the boy ran off to the bedroom, sobbing. Later on, John Y. told me that that was the reason he bought the whole franchise: "I could see little boys all over the city of Louisville crying like that," he said.

Buying the team and keeping it in Louisville was a noble thing for him to do but probably not a very smart business move. He was losing a great deal of money.

After I got back from Japan, John told me he wasn't going to trade me but might have to do something else—but he didn't say what. The stories about me being traded continued to crop up in the paper and, frustrated, I called David Vance, who was running the Colonels for John Y.

"If they're not true," I said to Vance, "then I want these rumors denied."

"Dan, I don't know if it's a rumor," he said. That really woke me up.

A couple of nights later I was at Louisville Downs, a harness track, along with Cheri and Sheridan. I was joking around with Stewart Jay about the whole situation when he said something odd. "You know, this might be one of those situations where the parts are worth more than the whole," Stewart said. Then he went on to suggest a unique scenario: that Artis and Louis and myself go out and sell ourselves to the highest bidder in the NBA. "You'd make a ton of money," he said.

At just about that point in our conversation, I got paged to take a phone call in the press box. Getting phone calls at a racetrack is practically unheard of because it requires special clearance. On the phone I heard the voice of Ellie Brown, John Y.'s wife at the time and the president of the Colonels. She wasn't calling to wish me happy birthday.

"Dan," she said, "this is the hardest thing I've ever had to do. But you've been traded to the Baltimore Claws."

"Ellie are you aware that I have a no-trade clause in my contract?" I said.

She said, "I thought you and John had that all worked out."

I said, "We don't have anything worked out."

And she said, "John, you'd better get on the extension."

That evening was one of the most bizarre times of my life. We left the track immediately and drove to Bruce Miller's house. You know how they always run the weather warnings across the bottom of the TV screen during regular programming? Well, Cheri and I were sitting there watching TV when we saw a strip that read: "Dan Issel has been traded to the Baltimore Claws. Details at eleven."

At that point, I couldn't go home because my phone would be ringing like crazy. "You'd better stay here tonight," he said, "and we'll get up in the morning and make some decisions."

Cheri and I were all dressed up and Bruce was wearing shorts, a baseball hat, a white T-shirt, and no shoes. I wanted a beer, and Bruce didn't have any, so we headed out to the Seven-Eleven for a six-pack. Sheridan still needed a pacifier then to sleep, but we didn't have any of her stuff with us, so while at the store I grabbed a couple of pacifiers and a six-pack. And the man at the cash register looks at us, me in a coat and tie, Bruce in his shorts, as if we were nuts. "I don't know what kind of party you're having," he said, glancing at the beer and pacifiers, "but I wish I was invited."

Eventually, it would turn out to be my going-away party.

The rumors were true. My worst fears had been confirmed. We were leaving Louisville. For Baltimore.

We had just finished building a custom-made home in Louisville with all the conveniences for a tall person—7' doors, 11' ceilings, built-up sink, oversized tub. It took 13 months to build. So it was more than just getting traded or sold. For the first time in our lives, we were being uprooted from home. This, of course, is normal procedure for most pro athletes, but I had led too sheltered a life to understand that.

That night at Bruce's began a four-day cloak-and-dagger ordeal. I was staggered, hurt, and uncertain what to do. Part of me wanted to stay and fight the no-trade clause issue; another part of me wanted to leave and put it behind me. I was taking this very personally. I had always thought there couldn't be a pro basketball franchise in Kentucky without Dan Issel. I was growing up to the realities of life in a hurry.

Cheri, Bruce, and I flew out to Washington and met with the Baltimore Claw owners. They made it sound good and kept offering me more incentives in my contract. One of them was that we'd get comparable housing. That, of course, was impossible: there is no house in Baltimore comparable to anything in the state of Kentucky, period. Because it's in Baltimore.

On the other hand, there was John Y., losing money faster than he could fry chicken, even after having won the ABA championship. There was no reason to think the financial picture in Louisville would change or that John could keep it afloat. So we decided to accept the Baltimore deal. Instead of trading me, the Colonels sold me. And we were off for Chesapeake Bay.

The agreement we had about comparable housing in Baltimore turned out to be a sham. When Cheri went out to look at houses every day, she came home depressed because they kept showing her two-bedroom apartments. We cried ourselves to sleep every night.

They say that in order to grow you must experience pain. Well, we grew a lot. For the first time, I knew that if it came down to a friendship or business with an owner, business would win out everytime.

Thus, even though I had a no-trade clause in my contract, I wound up having to leave Louisville. John Y. Brown sold me to the Claws for somewhere between $350,000 and $500,000. He kept Artis Gilmore, he said, because he believed that his career would be longer. Which was another way of saying he thought Artis was a better player.

Funny part about it was that at the end of my rookie year Jerry Colangelo, owner of the Phoenix Suns, had wanted me to jump from the Louisville ABA team to his NBA franchise—for a lot of money, three times what I was making with the Colonels. He tells me to this day that he still has a copy of that contract in his drawer. I didn't do it because I loved Kentucky and, frankly, because if I did it I thought I would never be able to show my face around the Bluegrass State again. At the time, of course, I never dreamed that the Colonels would soon be out of business.

Just a word about the ABA:
Those of us who helped pioneer it will always have a special place in our hearts for the red, white, and blue basketball. We were the founders of the three-point play, and we had some great players who are still going strong today in the NBA.

We knew what we were. At first the league was NBA rejects and old AAU players. By the time I got there, the ABA had been operating for three years and was beginning to attract some top talent. There will always be a common bond among the players, coaches, and owners who worked and played together in the ABA.

We think of those as the good old days. Of course, we forget about the bad times, tending to block out such things as the horrendous travel schedule of the ABA—having to sit in those coach seats with long legs, making five stops between Louisville and Greensboro on the way to playing the Carolina Cougars, for instance.

Nonetheless, in the heads and hearts of people like Artis or Julius Erving or George Gervin, you will find a special affection for the ABA. None of us, to a man, really believes that the league got the proper recognition. And it's sort of what diehard Southerners feel about the Civil War: "We didn't lose the war, we just ran out of supplies."

The ABA ran out of money.

My "feud" with John Y. Brown has been cussed and discussed over the years. A lot of people are under the impression that I hate the man, but I don't. I went through a period when I was very bitter toward him for what he did to me and my family. But that was probably my fault; I was totally naive about the ways of business. After all, I felt as if I was still playing for the University of Kentucky without attending the classes.

It's true that I didn't like John Y. for a long time after that. Actually, that's an understatement; I didn't like him the way Denver Bronco fans don't like the Los Angeles Raiders. But I was raised that holding grudges is wrong and that bitterness poisons the soul. Eventually, I had to deal with those feelings.

There is no such thing as having a friendship between player and owner these days, even though I was foolish enough to think it was possible with John Y. and myself. It didn't work between Reggie Jackson and George Steinbrenner either for various reasons. It didn't work between us because the franchise was never a money maker and was proving to be an unaffordable luxury.

You hear and read a lot about players being traded and sold. Today, in sports like baseball, where there is so much turnover with free agency, athletes change uniforms and cities like they change socks. It wasn't that way for me. My loyalties ran deep. In the beginning I was able to choose my town and my team. I never thought about playing for another team, which is why I turned down more than $300,000 a season to play for Phoenix. That decision not to jump to the NBA wound up costing me a lot of money—money that I would never recover.

Looking back on it now, I can see that the decision to sign with the ABA before the NBA draft and not to jump over to the NBA with Phoenix probably cost me more than a couple of million dollars. But I never learn. Even in my last three years, when the Nuggets were having financial problems, I accepted their offer without even testing the waters of free agency. Denver was where I wanted to play, even if it meant less money. And it did.

In my peak earning years, I made $600,000 as a Nugget. Backup centers on other teams were making a lot more.

Despite that, and despite the nightmarish experience of

Baltimore, I have never regretted choosing the ABA and the Kentucky Colonels. For one thing, at least I was able to earn a championship ring for 1975.

I also earned my spurs. During those 10 days in Baltimore, I did a lot of growing up.

Meanwhile, John Y. was getting heat from the fans and heat from the media.

The Baltimore Claws needed some of everything—recognition, press, support, players. I was meant to give them some credibility and to give John Y. some money. Except that ABA Commissioner Dave DeBusschere, current Knicks executive and former Knicks star, was so quick to pawn off the bankrupt Memphis Tams franchise, he didn't bother checking on the credit status of the future owners. Pretty soon, it became evident that the whole deal was shaky. John wasn't getting his money, and he was getting a lot of negative publicity.

Oddly enough, we found ourselves needing each other.

I was miserable in Baltimore and wanted out on the first train out of town. I began to check around the league and found out that the Denver Nuggets needed a center, for Marvin Webster had contracted hepatitis.

John Y. called. (It seems like every time I get in some foreign land like Japan or Baltimore, I get these telephone calls about my future.) This time John wanted to make a deal *with* me, not for me. He said that if I would make a statement of some kind to get the press off his back about shipping me to Baltimore, he'd do his best to get me in a better situation. Of course, he wasn't getting his money from the Claws anyway, so he had nothing to lose.

I agreed. It was one of the few times in my career that I actually used the media for my benefit. I've forgotten, now, what I said to soften the blow, but I would have told them John Y. was my natural father if it got me out of Baltimore.

We got a call shortly after that from Carl Scheer telling us that I had been sent to the Nuggets for Dave Robisch and cash. Denver sounded like heaven. They had to put some window dressing on the trade: Robisch went to Baltimore for a few days to make it look real, but in reality there was no trade. The money never went to the Claws; it went straight from Denver to Kentucky.

In Baltimore, they were still trying to keep the franchise afloat, but the Claws didn't have much pinch. They played three games and folded. I got one paycheck from the Claws and used it to open my bank account in Denver. It bounced.

I remember that Bruce Miller used that check in a collage he made for me of that entire experience. He wrote a letter to the sports editor of the *Baltimore Sun*, asking for a picture of me in a Claws uniform. The reply he got back was priceless: "I have tried to honor your request, to get a picture of Dan Issel in a Baltimore Claws uniform. But I don't think there ever was a picture made. And everybody connected with the Baltimore Claws franchise has disappeared like yesterday's thunderstorm."

The letter writer had a way with words. The whole ordeal was indeed a thunderstorm. But at least it was followed by a rainbow.

When John Y. Brown first ran for governor, he called and asked me if I would make a statement on his behalf. I really agonized over the decision of whether or not to do it, since it was nearly four years after the whole ordeal. So I called my father and asked him what I should do.

My father has always had wonderful conventional wisdom. He is a man of principle, a Christian man, and even though I'm sure he was unhappy with John Y. for shipping me off to Maryland, he was very objective. He told me: "You might be bitter about it now and dislike what the man did to you. But in the long run, it turned out to be the best thing for you. That was apparently the way it was supposed to happen. And you can't carry a grudge forever."

I realize now that John Y. meant nothing personal by trading me, but at the time I was crushed. After listening to my dad's advice, I went ahead and did the commercial for John Y.'s campaign, and he was elected.

After all our ups and downs, John and I remain good friends.

I know that he was trying to make an unemotional business decision and, now that I'm in the horse business, I see how tough that can be. Every now and then I run into Governor Brown at parties. I suppose I should actually thank him: while Baltimore wasn't the garden spot of America, Denver turned out to be a tremendous place to live and play. In the long run, things worked out for the best.

It took me 10 years to finally get back to Kentucky, to the land and the people that I love. It will always be home.

Sometimes I have wondered why it couldn't have worked, why the Colonels couldn't have survived. Expecially since the people of this state are so crazy about basketball. Reflecting on it now, I can see that there never was a big enough season ticket base. The market isn't large enough to support both the Kentucky Wildcats and a pro team right up the road. And college basketball is still king in these hills.

Plus the fact that the ABA drawing power wasn't exactly overwhelming. We had some great players, as I said, but we also had to carry some lightweights in our league.

One of them played for the Carolina Cougars and was named Doug Moe. He was eventually going to be my coach in Denver, after Larry Brown and Donnie Walsh. There is nothing on the face of this earth that can prepare you for Doug Moe. If Coach Rupp was "the Man in the Brown Suit," then Doug Moe has to be "the Man in the Clown Suit."

"

In Denver, we have something known as the Brown Cloud, the pollution that hangs over the city. Around McNichols Sports Arena, we have the Blue Cloud. It comes from all the profanity Doug uses in a single game.

"

8
THE MAN IN THE CLOWN SUIT
DOUG MOE

Strap on your seatbelt. If you're not familiar with the flamboyant, controversial, iconoclastic, wacko coach of the Denver Nuggets, then you simply won't believe anything in these next few pages.

Everything in this chapter is authentic, not fictional. Those who know Doug Moe can verify it. Those who don't will either have to trust me or look it up. And if you really want to read a zany book about basketball, wait until Moe writes his. It would make a great Alfred Hitchcock movie, starring Nick Nolte, a Moe lookalike.

I should warn you not to misinterpret my comments about Doug Moe as cheap-shot tactics. I actually love the guy and loved playing for him. But unless you insult Doug he doesn't think you love him. So when you are speaking to or about him there is a special language you must embrace in order for the big stiff to understand it.

A first and last serious comment about Doug: you could make a good case for him being the most underrated coach in the NBA. He gets remarkable results out of his material with an unorthodox coaching style.

You could also make a case for Doug being a raving lunatic.

Which one of the following statements about Doug Moe is not true?

- He once shot free throws left-handed in an ABA game after missing three in a row right-handed.
- He was idolized in Italy as a great basketball player, revered on the same level as Oscar Robertson and Jerry West.
- He was once fined and later suspended for throwing a cup of water on an NBA referee.
- He was once fined for instructing his Denver players not to play defense in the final 72 seconds of an NBA game at Portland.
- On NBA draft day, when other coaches were sending out wires as to their whereabouts, he sent a telex saying he could be reached on the ninth tee at a local golf course.
- Often he flies in a separate plane from his players, especially if their chartered course is scheduled to take them through the slightest bit of bad weather.
- He was once so frustrated with the officials in a game that, while walking to the locker room at halftime, he picked up an opposing player and lifted him off the floor as a gesture of protest.
- He was blackballed by the NBA because while in college he was offered a bribe, turned it down, and failed to report the bribe attempt.

Which statement about Doug Moe is untrue?
None.
I told you to fasten your seatbelt. The life story of Doug Moe is a roller-coaster ride you'll never forget.

In Denver, we have something known as the Brown Cloud, the pollution that hangs over the city. Around McNichols Sports Arena, we have the Blue Cloud. It comes from all the profanity Doug uses in a single game.
"%#@!!?**#!!+" is just a normal quote from Doug when he

talks to his players—at about 10,000 decibels. Doug is the Mad Screamer. Sooner or later he gets everybody, but he usually picks out one or two guys to be his favorite whipping boys. The smaller guys. Those who he knows can't physically hurt him.

Big guys like Calvin Natt and T. R. Dunn are accused of being his favorite players because he never yells at them. He never yells at them because Doug knows they will punch his lights out. Once, during a game in 1985, Doug was railing at Calvin to move up on defense. Without taking his eyes off his defensive man, Calvin said: "Shut up, Doug!" And Doug shut up.

How much he yells at you also depends on your personality and your status with the club. It can be very destructive. I remember Dave Robisch got screamed at as much as anybody, and I think it affected his game. Finally, one day Dave was at the free-throw line and Doug was standing up, yelling. Robo turned around and said: "Sit down and shut up." Doug did.

Another time he was simply ripping Alex English apart. Finally, as Alex came by the bench, he said to Doug: "If I'm so bad, Doug, take me out." So Doug did what he had to do: he took Alex out. For about 30 seconds.

Rookies can be devastated. Pro basketball under Doug Moe is a totally different experience from college basketball. They come from an environment of strict discipline, where coaches are father figures, into this, where some guy with tousled hair and wild eyes is breathing fire on their necks. The only similarity to this game and one that they played in college is that the ball is round and you shoot it through a hoop.

It's like walking through a forest and suddenly being met by a roaring lion: you don't know whether to run and hide, fight back, or just stand there and take it. Pretty soon, you learn by watching that if you yell back occasionally, Doug will lay off. He's unmerciful to the guy who just sits there and takes it.

Like Kiki Vandeweghe. Poor Kiki was the butt of Doug's wrath for years. Doug was trying to make Kiki mad so that he'd become more aggressive on the floor, but the tactic seldom worked. Kiki was his docile self and would stand there with that hang-dog look while Doug lit into him. Doug explained to Terry Frei of *The Denver Post* why he did it:

"I want him to tell me, '[Bleep] you,' " Doug said. "I want him to get mad enough to where it hurts him, to where he wants to knock somebody's ass off. He can do it. But just because it's his lifestyle, his personality. . . . I understand his personality makes it difficult for him to do certain things. Until he gets mad, though, he doesn't get after it."

Kiki played at UCLA and is California laid back. Doug is Brooklyn pushy. They just never could communicate totally, but Doug was responsible for helping develop Kiki into the great player he is today for the Portland Trail Blazers.

Actually, Doug's yelling is somewhat out of character, because everything else in his coaching repertoire is so unorthodox and relaxed. And he actually hates himself the next day for chewing out a guy in front of the entire crowd at McNichols Sports Arena. He's just a schizophrenic, that's all, and one of his personalities makes him into a screaming maniac at times during a game. Yet he is genuinely embarrassed by being that way.

Ron Zappolo, sports anchorman for KCNC-TV (Channel 4), does a great impersonation of Doug, frantically bouncing up and down the sideline, hands in his hair, screaming: "Alex! Alllllllexxxxx! Alex! Alllllllleexxxx!" Nobody laughs harder than Doug when he sees Ron's bit. But when Doug sees himself on TV doing that, he hangs his head in shame; he doesn't even want to watch. The truth is that until he sees it on TV, Doug doesn't even realize what he's done.

Sooner or later, you just have to learn to live with Doug's screaming. After a while, you wonder what's wrong if he doesn't.

As for the rookies, we veterans just take them aside and say: "If Doug yells at you, it's not because he doesn't like you or that he's trying to embarrass you. He just wants you to be a better ball player."

Don't get the impression that Doug can't be a very effective

Doug Moe, eat your heart out.

Back in the days of "Rupp's Runts," we were *all* big white stiffs.

About the rumor that Coach Rupp made a deal with me so that I could become Kentucky's all-time leading scorer—it's true.

A quick commercial for the University of Kentucky: for anyone who is serious about basketball, I think it's the best place in the country to go to school.

Before I met Coach Rupp for the first time, Joe B. Hall, then an assistant, gave me this advice: "If he doesn't laugh, don't you laugh. He'll say something you think is dumb, but if he laughs, you laugh too."

We never won the Final Four, but we did walk away with a couple of SEC Championships.

That's Scott. He's definitely not ready to play center, but maybe point guard.

For a kid who couldn't make the Little League team, threw worse than a girl, and couldn't make the high school frosh basketball team, I guess I did okay.

Some people might have thought I was stupid to sign with the ABA, but those of us who helped pioneer it—Julius Erving, George Gervin, Artis Gilmore—will always have a special place in our hearts for the red, white, and blue basketball.

I loved playing for the Kentucky Colonels, so I was a little upset when one night a bulletin flashed across the TV screen that read, "Issel Traded to Baltimore Claws. Details at eleven."

Don't let Doug's tuxedo fool you. The man owns two ties and two pairs of pants: brown for home games and blue on the road. "Most coaches couldn't do it," says Doug. "They'd get confused and wear brown on the road or blue at home."

Above: Any athlete who says he doesn't hear catcalls and boos is lying, and I'd sure be lying if I said all the boos I heard before I announced my retirement didn't hurt. **At right**: I didn't know I had lost my starting role at center until a used-car salesman asked me how I felt about it.

At upper left: Now that I'm a free man, I can spend more time with my real loves, my family and my horses. **At left**: My own championship team, filming a commercial for the Special Olympics. **Above**: The Issel Family—Sheridan, Scott, Dad, and Cheri.

Mr. Issel with his good friends Mr Travaglina, alias "Chopper," and Mr. Iacino, alias president of the Orange Crush distributorship in Denver.

I scored my 20,000th on the road, so the folks in Denver waited
until I came home to celebrate.

comunicator. He can. He knows when to pat you on the back and when to have his little heart-to-heart talks with you. But now I'm getting complimentary about him, and I promised I wouldn't.

Doug is one of the laziest people on the face of the earth.

I believe it was Donnie Walsh, Doug's friend and former head coach of the Nuggets who was also later Doug's assistant, who once said of Doug's college career: "Doug was so lazy, if he heard they were handing out A's over at the administration building, he'd ask somebody to drop by and pick him up a couple."

Doug's idea of a big night out is taking his wife, Jane, to some movie—it doesn't matter which one or how bad the reviews were—or going to the dog track to bet on the greyhounds. Thank God for Big Jane. If he didn't have her, he'd be a lost soul in the wilderness. And I think the only time she feels safe about Doug walking out of the house is on game nights. At least then she knows for sure where he's going and what he's doing.

On the road, Doug's intinerary is very predictable, never very ambitious. He spends all day in the hotel coffee shop. Some guys do museums; Doug does coffee shops. Being from the East, he has that "diner mentality." When Bill Ficke was the assistant coach, he'd get Doug out to a movie three or four times a year. But usually they'd sit in the coffee shop all day. I've seen them have two meals at the same table without ever getting up—breakfast and then lunch. Maybe play a few hands of gin in between, read the paper. Doug would never think of doing anything the least bit intellectually stimulating, like reading a book.

Maybe Doug has the right idea about pro basketball. Maybe we all do take ourselves too seriously. When you get right down to it, we are not deciding world policy and what we are doing isn't going to become the focal point of any history books. It is entertainment and you ought to have a good time, along with the people you entertain.

Maybe, in fact, Doug ought to go ahead and wear a clown suit when he's on the bench coaching. It might be an improvement over his current wardrobe. He owns two ties but only wears them at games because it's a club rule. He wears two colors of pants—brown and blue. In the spring of 1985, when ABC's Dick Schaap did a network piece on Doug, Schapp introduced Doug by saying, "Denver is a team that doesn't really have a superstar. In fact, it barely has a coach." Then there was Doug in his wrinkled brown pants, doing his self-deprecating bit: "It's easy. I wear brown pants at home, blue on the road. But most coaches couldn't do it. They'd get confused and wear brown on the road or blue at home."

Doug's wardrobe can best be described as a combination of late-fifties Robert Hall and early-eighties K-Mart.

Doug's favorite pasttime is lampooning his own profession. He constantly sticks the needle in other coaches, but he also does a number on himself: "I know what I am—slightly above a moron."

His favorite targets are guys like Hubie Brown, coach of the Knicks, and Jack Ramsay of the Portland Trail Blazers. They are two of the more cerebral types, both excellent coaches, and they spend a great deal of time talking basketball theory. Both are sticklers for detail. To Doug, detail is having to show up for games.

I'll bet you Hubie Brown has 400 different plays. I doubt we had more than four. But, as I said before, that's misleading. Doug coaches the passing game, and the passing game is predicated on reaction by the player to the ball. It's impossible to have set plays all the time with the passing game, which I think is a very effective offense. Doug, of course, doesn't ever say that; he just pretends to roll the balls out on the court and says, "Let's go, fellas."

Hubie and Doug once had a long-standing feud, but they kissed and made up in 1985 when Hubie was doing the color for the CBS telecasts of our series with the Lakers. In a *Sports Illustrated* article, Doug had criticized Hubie as "overrated" and for overcoaching. The truth of the matter is that Doug was mad at Hubie because of some things he'd said about two of Doug's good friends, Billy Cunningham of the 76ers and John MacLeod of the Suns. It was Doug's way of evening the score.

When Hubie blew into town, they glossed it over. "I have never said anything derogatory about Doug Moe," Brown told Bobby Van Winkle of *The Denver Post.* "I never mentioned the *Sports Illustrated* article. He said some things about me in the article, but I didn't say anything about him."

Doug, uncharacteristically, dodged the issue with: "There were a couple of things we said a couple of years back, but it's no big deal."

In that case, Doug copped out. He doesn't cop out, though, when it comes to making remarks about other coaches' material. Cotton Fitzsimmons of the San Antonio Spurs made the mistake of saying Denver should be favored in the playoffs. Doug responded by calling the Spurs "the most underachieving team in the history of the league." Moe was critical of how Fitzsimmons handled George Gervin, the great scorer. "They have hurt themselves with Gervin by telling him how old he is. And Gervin could have had such a great year," Doug said to *The Post.*

Then Doug helped out his friend Bill Fitch of the Houston Rockets by saying before the season started that they were "the team of the future" and would win 50 games. They didn't, of course.

You can never accuse Doug of being partial, though. Sometimes he's harder on himself than any other coach in the league.

Part of Doug is a pussycat. When you eat lunch with him, or talk with him after a game, or just have a beer, he is an unassuming, fun-loving guy who very rarely talks about himself or tries to dominate a conversation. Yet he is so fiercely competitive that the Doug Moe on the sideline is transformed into a zealot.

He will go to war in a second, especially if it involves a basketball official. Over the years, Doug has engaged in more wars with referees than the Israelis have with the Arabs.

Back in 1979, when Doug was coaching the San Antonio Spurs, he accused officials Paul Mihalak and John Vanak of "stealing the game" after the Spurs were eliminated from the playoffs by the Washington Bullets, 107–105. Commissioner Lawrence O'Brien socked Doug with what was then the largest fine ever handed down to an NBA coach—$3,000.

That, however, did not deter Doug from his appointed wars with the zebras. In 1983, Doug got mad at Tommie Wood, a substitute official scabbing for the striking NBA referees, so he threw a cup of water on Tommie. For that little trick, they tossed him out of the game—an automatic $500 fine—and then the NBA tacked on $3,000, plus a two-game suspension. I was standing right next to him when it happened, and I thought he was going to be suspended for the whole season.

I think Doug has gotten a little more selective in his battles with the refs. Now he knows which ones to scold, which ones to kid around with, and which ones to avoid altogether. Before, he treated them all the same: like dogs.

I mentioned before Doug's lax attitude toward time. The players finally convinced him to put in a fine system for tardiness in 1984. Guess who was the first guy hit with a $50 fine for being late—yep, Doug. He got to practice five minutes late the very first day.

At least he improved in my last season by showing up before games for the national anthem, although he gets uptight listening to it. "That," Doug says, "is the worst time."

I think Doug enjoys being aloof because it keeps the players off guard. He's liable to do most anything. One day after a particularly bad practice, Doug was trying to make a point by imitating the New Orleans Saints football fans who showed up at games wearing brown paper bags over their heads. Instead Doug put a clear plastic bag over his head, which wasn't too smart considering the risk of suffocation. He was intelligent enough to finally take it off.

That was the same week in which Doug was quoted in *Sports Illustrated* as saying Hubie Brown was "overrated" and the same day he told reporter Frei that he was changing his image. "Let's put it this way," Doug said. "I'm making somewhat of a conscious effort not to be perceived as completely off the wall. I used to say things like, 'To hell with practice, let's go to Vegas.' Or, 'Let's go play golf.'

"I'd sit around with the press for two hours in San Antonio, then I'd say, 'I've got to go play golf.' Kidding, of course. Some other coach talks to the press five minutes and says, 'I've got a film meeting now.'

"So my image is bad. That shows you the power of the spoken word. And other coaches will tell me I'm making the coaching profession look bad. That's something I don't want to do, so I'm getting away from that."

In recent years, I think Doug has become aware of creating the wrong image. He realizes now that some people take him seriously when they shouldn't. I just hope he never changes to the point of losing that fun-loving, cavalier, attitude when he's not on the bench coaching. Sometimes a good laugh at the expense of Doug was all that kept me going.

The two incidents most damaging to Doug's reputation were both done with good intentions. In both cases, he was implicated for impugning the integrity of basketball.

If he were honest about it, Doug would probably admit to wishing he could have back that night of November 22, 1983. That's when he instructed us to lay down against the Trail Blazers in the final 72 seconds, not to impede their scoring. They went on to a record 156-point night.

At the time, that incident didn't seem too radical. We were already getting blown out by nearly 40 points, and Doug was furious because our defense had been so poor. So he called a 20-second time-out and told us to lay off because we hadn't been playing defense anyway. He was trying to make a point.

The NBA got the point and Doug got the fine, this time $5,000 and a two-game suspension. Scotty Stirling of the NBA said

Doug was "making a travesty" out of the league and "seriously tarnishing the image." You could make a case for Doug "tarnishing the image" of basketball when he's just standing there, being his normal, sloppy self. But that's not what they were talking about. They were suggesting that Doug was hurting the reputation of basketball as an honest game.

The NBA made it sound as if Doug were shaving points, but the outcome of the game wasn't going to be affected. Looking back on it now, I can see why the league would be concerned about a team that didn't score every time it could or didn't attempt to stop the other team from scoring every trip down the court. But when it happened, I didn't consider Doug in the wrong or give it much thought at all.

That incident wasn't as damaging, though, as the one that had occurred when Doug was attending the University of North Carolina.

Aaron Wagman, a gambler who would ultimately become a convicted fixer, met with Doug in New York during the summer of 1960 and asked him to shave points in games the next season. Doug refused, but he took $75 from Wagman for expenses back to Chappel Hill, North Carolina, and he failed to report the attempted bribe.

Doug was nailed for that.

"I thought I had done a good thing," said Moe, "in turning the guy down." But it came out in testimony that both Tony Jackson of St. John's University and Doug failed to report the attempted bribe, and both Doug and Jackson were blackballed by the NBA. Doug was "suspended" from North Carolina after he had already finished his eligibility but hadn't yet graduated. Eventually, Doug was vindicated by a lawsuit against the NBA, which was settled out of court for a rather large sum of money.

The NBA doors were slammed, but a whole new vista was opened for Moe as a basketball player in Europe. He might have been a black sheep in America, but Doug became a hero in Italy.

Donnie Walsh, who played with Doug at North Carolina,

recalled for *The Denver Post* the correspondence he had with Doug when he was playing in Italy: "He used to send us clippings and the headlines would say 'El Grandioso Moe.' And he was the best. Compare him to Jerry West, Oscar Robertson, all those guys. That was about the same time Bill Bradley went over there, too, and I knew Doug was better than Bradley."

I never got to see Doug in his prime. When I played against him, Doug didn't have a lot of talent, but he tried hard. Of course both knees were gone then and he was getting near the end of his career. My father-in-law saw him play in college and said Doug was one of the best he ever saw. His personality on the court was 180 degrees from the way he was in person: Doug would go 100 miles an hour on the court, but off the court, as I've said, Doug is basically a lazy guy.

When looking at coaches and deciding what they'd be doing if they weren't coaching basketball, I'd say Jack Ramsay of Portland would probably be a college professor. Dick Motta of Dallas would be a business executive. Doug would be a race-track tout.

It's only fair to discuss a little of the other side of Moe, even though I promised I wouldn't be too complimentary—I come to bury Doug, not praise him. But in the interest of balance, let me repeat that he is one helluva basketball coach.

On game day, give me Doug Moe running the team on the bench. When you throw the basketball up, nobody wants to win more than Doug. He knows how to make adjustments during the game, usually senses a good rotation for substitutes, keeps in the flow of the game, and can inspire a team at the proper time. The rap on him is that he doesn't have set plays in the final minutes. I think Doug knows exactly what he wants to do late in the game and how to get the ball to the right person. He may not draw it up the same way Hubie Brown or Jack Ramsay does, but he gets the job done. And that's what counts.

He's a much better coach than he gets credit for. He was runnerup as NBA Coach of the Year in 1985, and I think he should have won it instead of Don Nelson of Milwaukee. To win

52 games and the division with the talent we had took great coaching. And he did it in a clutch situation, when Nugget management was looking for any reason to throw him over the side.

It was so enjoyable playing for Doug because he could separate the personal from the professional side. I've played for coaches who take it as a personal affront when a player has a bad night or makes a stupid play, and they won't talk to the player for three days. With Doug, when the game is over, he can still be your friend. You might go out and get a beer and a sandwich together and whether you've played great or poorly he enjoys being with you.

A lot of coaches have a system and they play that system whether they've got 12 giants or 12 midgets; even when they don't have the right kind of talent, they hammer the players and try to make them fit into it. But Doug adjusts his style to the talent at hand. There is no better evidence of that than when he had a front line of Kiki Vandeweghe, Alex English, and Dan Issel. Who are you going to guard? The only way to play is to run and gun.

I love that style of play, and Doug loved it, too. Two days after we set the all-time scoring record in the 186–184 loss to Detroit, Doug said he would have liked to see us reach the 200-point level. "That would have been terrific" he said. "That would have been a classic." Once again the maverick Moe had embarrassed his fellow coaches by breaking down another barrier with a 370-point game. I've always wondered if he wasn't getting back at the league for fining him over the Portland incident.

Doug swears he would never walk the ball up the court and slow down the pace, but I'll bet you that if he had a bunch of 6'11" players he would. He'd do whatever it took to win. That's why I think he's a good coach. People say he can't coach defense—hell, he never had any players who could play defense.

In 1984, it certainly didn't look like Doug was the choice of

Vince Boryla to coach the Nuggets. On the day of the press conference announcing Vince's appointment as president of the team, reporters tried to get a vote of confidence out of him. Vince wouldn't budge.

Here, from the files of *The Denver Post*, is how Vince dodged the issue:

Question: "Will Doug Moe be with the team?"

Boryla: "Oh, yeah, sure. Doug's here."

Question: "Moe will be here next season?"

Boryla: "Business as usual covers it all."

Question: "Can you just say 'yes'?"

Boryla: "Business as usual."

Question: "So Doug will be here?"

Boryla: "It's business as usual. I'm here until I'm not here. I'm not here forever. The owner [then Red McCombs] might call up every day to see if I'm here. I don't know. It's business as usual. He's here."

The "business as usual" turned out to be a string-along which caused a strained relationship for the next few months. Vince claims now that he "never had any problems with Doug," that it was just a matter of time before they sat down and worked out a contract. That's not quite how it was. Vince was already thinking about possible replacements, including a college coach, but before he could find a good candidate, the Nuggets were out of the box with a 12–2 start in the fall of 1984.

Eventually Doug got a new contract, but only after there was a big hassle in the Denver media for months. Doug and Vince fell short of negotiating in the press, but clearly the sportswriters and sportscasters were in favor of Doug getting a new contract. During that time, rumors were still swirling around about Doug's possible dismissal. At one point it turned into a death watch for Doug. "I don't know," Doug said, "maybe it's like they say: 'The husband is the last to know.' "

Doug didn't press the Nuggets on money, and at the first opportunity he went in and signed a new contract without really negotiating. According to printed reports, he got a contract worth $275,000 a year, plus incentives. That sounds like a lot, but keep in mind that it's still more than $25,000 less than the average player's salary and only about $60,000 more than the average coach's. For a guy with the fifth-best record among active NBA coaches, that's not exactly striking the mother lode.

They ought to pay Doug $100,000 a year just to fly in airplanes because he's so paranoid about it.

One thing Doug and I share is that both of us are uncomfortable in planes. But I have to admit that he's worse. When he was a player, sometimes he'd get off the plane when it made a stop and drive the rest of the way.

He's not a drinker—a beer now and then—but sometimes he'll have a Bloody Mary just after takeoff. Then he walks up and down the aisles of the plane, talking to anybody who will talk to him about anything they want to discuss, to keep his mind off the flight.

If he got up in the morning, turned on the weather channel, and saw that there was a thunderstorm between Denver and our destination, he would wait and take an afternoon flight. There were several times my last year when he turned around and went home from the airport.

He'll never take a wide-body plane, and it got to the point where the team's trainer and traveling secretary, Chopper Travaglini, was booking our flights around Doug's likes and dislikes. One day Chopper said, "This is ridiculous. We're taking flights two hours earlier in the morning just to avoid certain planes." So he stopped adjusting just for Doug, and now Doug sometimes doesn't fly with the team.

One quirk of my own about flying is that I have to sit next to a window so I can see out. If I can see either the tops of clouds or the ground, I'm a great flyer. But if we're in the clouds or flying at night when I can't see anything, I'm a terrible flyer. At my worst, though, I'm not as bad as Doug. One day I expect to read that Doug has decided to join John Madden on the trains, although that might make it a little tough for him to get from Salt Lake City one night to Boston the next.

Doug is an asset to the team in many ways, but one of the biggest is that he is a darling of the media. Being as quotable and as colorful as he is, Doug probably gets as much ink as Dan Reeves of the Broncos—which is remarkable considering the popularity of the Broncos. But the Denver media are worth a whole chapter in themselves.

That's one nice thing about writing a book. You get to even the score with some of the media people.

9
BRONCOMANIA AND THE MEDIA
IS THERE LIFE AFTER FOOTBALL IN DENVER?

Coming from Louisville via Baltimore, there was no way Denver was going to look bad to me. All I knew about the Mile High City was what I'd heard in John Denver's lyrics and what little I'd seen on the few trips there to play the Nuggets. You never get the correct impressions of a city when you're an athlete on a visiting team passing through town. You see the airport, the ballpark, stadium, or basketball arena, and the hotel. You don't feel the pulse or heartbeat of a city or experience the soul of the people.

Back in Kentucky, people think everything west of Kansas City is cowboy boots, cowboy hats, and big belt buckles. I had no clue what a nice town Denver was and what a great sports city it would turn out to be.

Nor was I prepared for the media blitz that was forthcoming.

All of us have read stories about the horrible experiences of athletes in New York back when there were a dozen or so newspapers there. They say the pressure of the press on Roger Maris was so intense in 1961, when he was chasing Babe Ruth's record of 60 home runs, that large chunks of his hair fell out. I can't imagine what it must have been like for people like Maris, or Joe DiMaggio during his 56-game hitting streak, or even Tom

Seaver and the 1969 Mets. But I can tell you this: no other city in America these days has more intense competition for sports coverage than Denver.

It seems that the biggest battle of the newspaper war involving *The Denver Post* and the *Rocky Mountain News* is waged between the sports departments. There is a premium on sports news, and that means reporters are constantly watching everything sports figures do and listening to everything they say. Stories that would never see the light of day in a one-newspaper town are printed regularly in Denver. I must say that as a sports fan, I enjoyed that. As a pro athlete, sometimes it was a pain. Fortunately, my relationship with the media has always been excellent, but there were times when my patience was definitely tested.

Overkill was fairly common between the two sports departments of the leading newspapers, especially when it involved the Denver Broncos. When they played the Seattle Seahawks in what was billed as "the Battle at Seattle" in December 1984, more than 50 credentials were issued to Colorado newspapers, TV, and radio stations. I'm told that nearly half of those went to writers and photographers for *The Post* and the *Rocky Mountain News*. I'm also told that it is believed to be an NFL record for the size of a visiting press contingent to a regular-season game.

Besides *The Post* and *Rocky Mountain News*, papers from Boulder (*The Daily Camera*), Pueblo (*Chieftan*), and Colorado Springs (*Sun* and the *Gazette-Telegraph*) also have full-time beat reporters on the pro sports teams in Denver. This is in addition to the four TV Stations, KCNC, KWGN, KUSA, and KMGH. And what other city in the United States has three daily radio sports talk shows? Denver does, on radio stations KLAK, KNUS, and KOA.

That gives you a little taste of the Denver media, but that's like taking a bite of only the butter pecan at Howard Johnson's.

Denver is a young city, and sports tend to be more important to the yuppies, I guess. Therefore, a large segment of the media goes toward coverage of sports—primarily pro sports, for

Colorado collegiate sports have been on the decline since the late seventies.

The sports fan is the beneficiary of the newspaper war between the *Rocky Mountain News*, owned by Scripps-Howard, and *The Post*, owned by the Times-Mirror Corporation. Now that I'm back living in Lexington, I miss the broad coverage of the two Denver sports sections. I think the two Denver newspapers have sports sections as fine as those of any paper in this country.

Unfortunately, the vast majority of the media attention is focused on the Broncos. Not that the coverage of pro basketball in Denver is lacking—to the contrary, it's better than 98 percent of the NBA's cities, and I'd be hard-pressed to come up with that other 2 percent. Basketball in the sports pecking order just comes second to football everywhere, particularly in Denver. Always will. Broncomania to Colorado is what the Mormons are to Utah—a religion.

There was one time, when I first came to Denver, when the Nuggets were playing their last season in the ABA, that we at least challenged the Broncos for supremacy. In 1975, McNichols Sports Arena had just been built, we won the regular ABA season title for the second straight year, and attendance was excellent. The following season, in the fall of 1976, we joined the NBA and won the division. But nobody paid much attention because the Broncos were winning the AFC title and going to the Super Bowl. It became obvious then that no matter how successful the Nuggets were, Denver was a pro football town. That seemed to set the pattern, because even to this day, until the Bronco season ends, nobody gives the Nuggets much serious notice.

That's the way it was my final season. We started off with a 12–2 record, but by then the Broncos were sailing toward a 13–3 record and the Nuggets' attendance fell way off until January. By then the Broncos had been eliminated, losing to the Steelers in the first round of the playoffs. Only then did fans start coming out to watch basketball.

We could have been 14–0, playing in the nude, and still not have drawn anybody. No matter how good or bad we were, nobody was going to see us until the Bronco season was over.

On a Tuesday we could be playing one of the best teams in the league, but the headlined story on the lead sports page of both newspapers was about the Broncos, not the Nuggets. That's what people wanted to hear and read about.

It's like your first girlfriend or boyfriend: you never forget him or her. The fans of Denver have always had a special feeling for the Broncos, win, lose, or draw, because that was their first big-league sports franchise. Years ago, when Lou Saban was coach, the fans went door to door to collect enough money so that the Broncos could stay in business. Today they have a waiting list of 15,000 for season tickets, the longest in the NFL, and going into the 1985 season had sold out 109 straight home games at 75,100 capacity.

One reason I was a Bronco fan myself was that I couldn't escape it, whether reading the newspapers, turning on the TV, or listening to the radio. Denver radio is saturated in the afternoon with dialogue about sports.

I suppose my favorite show was "Irv and Woody Sportstalk" on KLAK, now KRXY. Woody Paige who used to write a sports column for the *Rocky Mountain News* and then switched to *The Post*, was one of the original cohosts of the show. Woody has since given up sports for a news column and hosting a regular nonsports morning talk show on KNUS.

I particularly enjoyed Woody's writing, no matter what it was about, because he was entertaining. He was the first member of the media to call me when I was traded by the Claws, so maybe there's a little personal favoritism on my part. But whether I agreed with him or not, I always enjoyed reading his column. There are a lot of people who don't like him or his forthright, outspoken style, but I think Woody has something that many writers lack—a sense of humor. He could make me laugh. Even when he took a shot at me, it was done in a humorous sort of way. Maybe it's just that I understand his kind of humor—which, I suppose, ought to worry me.

The best "Irv and Woody" shows were the ones when they disagreed and got into it with each other. They were so completely different. Irv is a nice guy who sees nothing but good in everybody and everything; Woody is the complete opposite, seeing good in very few. The call-in show on KRXY had an unusually high caliber of callers, especially when Woody and Irv were together with Joe Williams. The callers weren't wishy-washy, and there were a lot of differences of opinion.

Irv is the only man I know who can have 45 restaurants as sponsors and tell you every day that each one of them is the best in Denver. Carl Scheer once said of Irv, "He never met a product he didn't like." There must be two or three of him, because he's everywhere. One minute he's on ESPN doing billiards, the next minute he's coming to you out of Omaha with the college World Series. Or he's on KRXY, selling you hot dogs and beer or Mexican food.

Over at KNUS, former Broncos Mike Haffner and Jim Turner call themselves "Sports SuperStars," which is a bit of a misnomer. (I wouldn't dare call myself a superstar while I was playing, let alone after I've been retired for a decade.) Mike and Jim are the non-boat rockers, and their show is mostly about football—and there wasn't much conversation about the Nuggets, so I didn't listen to them much. But I listened enough to know that Mike was a great one for changing his opinion in midstream. One guy would call in and say, "Dan Issel is a great player and the Nuggets are really going to miss him." And Mike would say, "Yes, you're right, Dan is an outstanding player." The next caller might say, "Issel is a stiff, he can't play a lick." And Mike would respond, "You're right, he can't jump, can't run, and can't rebound a lick." Mike has an opinion for every occasion. I'll give this to Haffner though: at least we would see him around the arena at Nugget games. But Jim Turner, to my knowledge, seldom attended a Nugget basketball game.

A guy we also saw a lot of was Bob Martin of KOA, the flagship station of the Nuggets. Bob is the number one radio personality in Denver, and has been for a long time. In addition to doing the play-by-play broadcasts of the Broncos while Larry Zimmer does color, Bob also alternates with Sandy Clough on the color of the Nugget broadcasts while Jeff Kingrey announces play-by-play.

Sometimes Bob hosts KOA Sportstalk, as do Clough, Kent

Groshong, and Kingrey, but it's a much more sophisticated show than the other two shows in town. The listeners calling in are not very knowledgeable about sports and tend to ask polite but silly or mundane questions.

KOA Sportstalk is more like the shows around Louisville and Cincinnati. I recently did a show with Tim Smile on Louisville station WVLK, after I retired. It was one of those where the callers would say, "Hi, Dan, how are you? It's good to have you back in Kentucky." Nice but not very interesting to the listener. I've never found, when I'm on a show, that people will call up and say, "Issel you're a real stiff! How did you ever play pro basketball so long without being exposed?" People don't want to confront you, which I guess is good manners.

Sometimes I think the hosts of the three radio call-in shows in Denver overanalyze situations. They get into stuff about the weakness of a team, maybe talk for hours about the lack of a kicking game or offensive rebounding. I don't think most fans care much about things like that. Denver is a town of mobile people—upwardly mobile— and most yuppies who move there either bring a favorite team with them or adopt the Broncos or Nuggets. Sometimes, as in the case of the Broncos, it's the snob appeal of having tickets. Basically, they want a team they can cheer for and support, and do not want to hear their teams dissected by some talk-show host infatuated with his or her own opinions.

So that's how I feel about the Denver media as Dan Issel the fan. But as Issel the player, it's a little bit different.

Handling the press can be a very delicate situation. I can honestly say that the only time I ever really tried to manipulate the media was when I told Woody Paige I might retire if the Nuggets didn't give me the money I'd wanted. To be perfectly honest, I wasn't going to retire, so I gave him some bum material. But I told him that and he wrote it. In my quest for leverage with the franchise, I was less than honest.

Some people might say that's part of the game. I feel a little ashamed of it, because I've benefited from excellent coverage in my career. But I don't think it's possible to change a writer's mind by telling him that something is black if it is white. If a writer has certain feelings to begin with, you might be able to substantiate them, but the media is too aware of what's going on to be manipulated to the point of writing something they don't believe or know to be true. I suspect that in this case with Woody he was going to bat for me because he felt I deserved the money. So I only substantiated what was already in his mind.

I can only think of one time that I got totally screwed by a newspaper reporter, and that was a guy named Kelly Dude— honest, that was his real name—of the *Rocky Mountain News*.

It was sort of like the Mike Evans thing, where the NBA salaries came out and Mike was the lowest-paid player in the league. In this case Kelly had gotten hold of some old information which incorrectly listed me as the lowest-paid center in the league at $180,000 a year. Actually, I had made that two years prior and, besides, that didn't include any of my perks or incentives. So that figure was wrong. If all the other salaries they had published were accurate, then maybe I was in the middle of the pack, but certainly not last.

Kelly came out to do an article on me while we were practicing at the old Court Club on South Broadway. My in-laws were flying in to visit and I had to get to the airport in a hurry. I was already late picking them up because I had taken some extra time to make certain I gave Kelly the information he needed. I explained to Kelly that the figure was old, that it didn't include such things as the Nuggets paying my mortgage or paying for my car or for my kid's private school. I didn't say, "Hell, no, Kelly, that's private information and I'm not going to tell you that."

What he wanted from me, of course, wasn't that factual stuff, but my reaction to being the lowest-paid center in the NBA. I couldn't give it to him, because I wasn't. The next day, when his story came out, it was pretty much a recitation of facts—except for the headline: "Issel Upset Over Being NBA's Lowest Paid Center," or something like that.

I rarely do this, but I confronted Kelly the next day and said,

"What's this garbage?" And he answered with the great cop-out that all the writers have: "I just write the story, somebody else writes the headlines." And I said to him, "Kelly, if my name was on the byline, I would make sure the headline was more accurate than that."

That's one of the few times I ever got angry with Carl Scheer, because he could have set the record straight by coming out with some facts. But I think it made him look good with the stockholders, so he kept quiet.

As for Kelly Dude, I didn't speak to him for a whole year. That's the only time I ever froze out a reporter like that, although I sure felt like doing it at other times. But it's very unwise to do that, because in the long run it hurts you, and then you have no forum.

I can see how Roger Maris started losing chunks of his hair. Maybe I can blame my receding hairline on the Denver press corps.

That's not to say I didn't enjoy the media, expecially the real pros, the ones who were competent and worked hard to do the job right. My favorites were usually the columnists, especially Woody Paige and Dick Connor of the *Rocky Mountain News*. I enjoyed reading their columns, whether they were on basketball or not, whether I agreed with their opinions or not.

I never cared for T. J. Simer's column in the *News*. He always seemed to be imitating Woody, and his opinions seemed hollow to me. He would take the opposite side of an issue just for the sake of argument. But I guess he accomplished what he set out to do, because I read him every morning along with the others, no matter what he wrote. In the final analysis, if the writers get you to read them, they have accomplished their goal.

Being a beat writer for a pro team would be extremely difficult. They travel on the same plane with the team, stay at the same hotel, eat at the same coffee shops, sometimes drink at the same bar. So it must be difficult to draw the line between what's personal and what's news. One writer who covered us for the *News*, Kevin Simpson, got the nickname "Scoop" because he would pretty much put everything that he saw or heard in the paper. Kevin has since left the *News* for *The Post* and no longer covers the Nuggets, but I think some of the players lost confidence in Kevin because of his reputation for printing everything.

Still, I think that the Nugget coverage by Kevin Simpson, when he was at the *News*, and Terry Frei of *The Post* may have been the most thorough of any while I played in Denver. They were always on top of what was going on and usually knew more than we knew.

I can't say that of the two beat writers for the two major dailies during my last season.

One, Teri Thompson of the *News*, had to overcome a lot of problems just to do her job, although she did it very competently. I felt sorry for Teri. She had to come in the locker room, which was often more uncomfortable for her than for us. She was the outsider; therefore, some guys weren't going to conform just for her. I'm from the old school—call me a sexist or whatever, but I don't think a woman should have to walk around a roomful of naked men in order to do her job. I always wrapped myself in a towel and at least took my underwear and clothes back into the room next to the shower, but there were a lot of guys who didn't do that; a lot of players just took off their uniforms and sat around in the nude as if there were no women in their presence. That's why I felt embarrassed for her many times.

Then there was Mark Kiszla of *The Post*. Sometimes I read his account of the game and I wondered if he'd seen the same one that I was playing in. And, of course, he and Teri were always playing cat and mouse.

I remember one day Teri came in the locker room and asked me to go outside, so I did. She was trying to dodge Mark, because they were both chasing the same story. "He's been following me around all day," she fumed. Just as she asked me about my retirement, which I hadn't yet announced, Mark's head popped around the corner.

Such is life in the newspaper war.

I have a lot of problems with some of the newer writers. Some of the young people coming up always seem to be digging for something negative. They think that's the only way to sell newspapers. Of course, I guess their bosses are actually to blame, because that's apparently what they're told to do.

The problem I had my final season with Teri and Mark, and the beat writers from other Colorado cities, was that I don't think they were fair to the guys on the team, or to the readers of their papers. When it came time to tell the public what types of individuals were on the team, they fell short. Rather than try to create controversy every day, why not sit down and try to write a story about the kind of person Calvin Natt really is? I know some of them complained that Calvin wasn't the easiest guy in the world to know and, admittedly, he shares that blame because the player has a certain obligation to fulfill, too.

Rather than being totally negative and doing the very thing I have criticized the Denver media for, however, let me say that, except for this one major flaw, I thought the coverage of the Nuggets by the print media when I was on the team was terrific. Just a quick note on some other print-media types I've encountered over my career.

- Dave Kindred of the *Atlanta Journal-Constitution* is an excellent writer. I knew him when he worked in Louisville, before he joined the *Washington Post* and ultimately moved to Atlanta. His horse-racing columns were among the best stuff I've ever read.
- Another guy I like is Barney Nagler, who writes the non-horse-racing stuff for *The Racing Form.*
- Blackie Sherrod of *The Dallas Morning News* is a favorite along with the Denver writers I've mentioned.
- And Billy Reed of the *Louisville Courier-Journal,* who worked in Lexington when I attended Kentucky, is a standout columnist.
- One guy I can't stand is Peter Vescey of the *New York Post.* He's one of those guys who digs up dirt on people so he can be controversial, a sort of Rona Barrett of the NBA. His style of writing, whether I agree or disagree with his position, is the equivalent to cheap-shot artists in the NBA.
- I'll admit to a personal prejudice against Jim Murray of the *Los Angeles Times*—and I'm going against my two criterion when I say this. Ever since he wrote some articles knocking

the Kentucky Derby, I haven't had much use for him. But he's a talented writer and obviously has the respect of his peers.

That's one nice thing about writing a book. You get to even the score with some of the media people.

Denver TV stations have their ratings wars, and it's gotten very competitive, but not to the extent that all four of them cover the Nuggets on a daily basis.

This is a biased assessment, because I've always been partial to Channel 4, KCNC. KCNC not only reports the sports in depth and at length but has a large staff that covers a wide variety of sports. But the real reason that I am biased is because Ron Zappolo, the sports anchor, is one of my closest friends in the city. Naturally I like his show the best.

Basketball happens to be one of Ron's passions. He hosts "The Doug Moe Show," as well as "The Dan Reeves Show" in Bronco season. What I appreciate the most about Ron is that he was always at the Nugget practice in the morning, even though he had to be anchoring the sports on the 10 o'clock news that night. It isn't easy for him to show up for a shoot-around on a Tuesday morning when we've got the Cleveland Cavaliers that night. But he was there. It took the excitement of the playoffs, if anything, to bring the other sports anchors out. That's why I think Ron was the most popular TV guy in Denver with the players—because he did his homework. And why he's also the best TV sportscaster in town.

Brian Drees of KMGH, Channel 7, is the second-best sportscaster in the city. He works hard and he adds stature to the KMGH sportscast. I also like Channel 7 sports' Steve Harms very much and got to know him better in the playoffs. Perhaps his schedule didn't permit him to be around the team as much as Ron, but I would have felt more comfortable talking to him in the playoffs if I had seen him during the regular season.

KMGH has also recently added Gary Cruz, formerly of KUSA, Channel 9, but you hardly ever saw either him or Mike Nolan of Channel 9 around the Nuggets.

Channel 2, KWGN, is an independent station which telecasts some of our games. Jim Conrad, who calls the play-by-play, is very capable, but his resources are limited. Jim often didn't have time to show up for many practices. For a small station I thought that KWGN did an admirable job covering our games. And I admired Channel 2's guts for doing the two-hour "Dan Issel Night" Cancer Society special.

We had a standard joke among the players: "Are the Michelins here yet?" we'd say, in reference to the members of the media who only came out when it was time to jump on the bandwagon. During the regular season, barely one press row was filled with the beat writers, columnists, and electronic media. Once the playoffs started, it took two rows just for the local press. I always called it "front-runners' row." *Sometimes* they would show up early. When the Bronco season was over and if we were off to a good year, they would actually come out before the playoffs started.

So you can see what it's like playing pro sports in Denver: a fish bowl. It's worse for the Broncos than for the Nuggets, but the fans make a lot of demands on both teams. With such intense coverage of sports by the local media it's hard not to be familiar to the public.

I was always very concerned about what the fans thought of me. I worked hard to develop a relationship with them, for it's not something that just happens; you have to work at it and earn it. I can't ever remember walking out of an arena and not signing an autograph for anyone who asked. I think the man (and woman) who puts the money down for the ticket is the reason we are able to make such a great living. So where some players feel that all they owe the fans is an honest effort on the court, I think it goes further. I think you should be civil to them and, if they want an autograph, oblige them.

The one time I did not do that was the time our first baby, Sheridan, was born, in 1972. It caused a big stink and I never was able to clear my name of it. I was playing for the Colonels, and we had a day game and she was born that afternoon. When the game ended, I hurriedly showered, dressed, and ran out of the dressing room on a bee-line for the hospital. There were lots of kids there that day, and I sort of pushed my way through them and kept going. A few days later, some woman who was apparently there with her kid wrote a letter to the *Courier-Journal.* It was a blistering letter that said I was conceited, that I refused to take time to sign autographs, and who did I think I was, anyway? She told me good. Obviously she had no idea of the circumstances.

So, after that, I tried to find the right balance and be aware of my public behavior because people don't always know the circumstances. A pro athlete is always going to make some people mad, regardless, and unless he wants to give up his family completely, there is no way to satisfy every fan's wish. But I don't think there was ever a situation where I didn't try to handle it nicely. There is never an excuse for being rude.

Sometimes, when I look back, I think perhaps there were times when I slighted my family and pushed them in the background just to oblige an autograph. Autographs are so funny, anyway. I've had people ask me for my autograph, look at it, and say, "Who are you?" or, "Who do you play for?" I think getting autographs is pretty dumb, unless you have a nice autograph book and it's something you want to save. For instance, I would love for Scott to have the autograph of the famous jockey Bill Shoemaker. But if Bill were sitting in a restaurant, about to have his entree, I would not send Scott over with a napkin for Bill to sign. When somebody does that, you know it's going to end up on a kitchen counter for a few days and eventually go in the trash.

Bill Russell said that giving somebody your autograph implies that you know them, which is why he never signed autographs. I wouldn't go that far. But, if I had it to do over again, I might not be so willing to inconvenience my family on a night out just to put my signature on a meaningless piece of paper.

However, I will never do what Larry Bird did to me one night when the daughter of a friend asked to be introduced to the Boston Celtic superstar. Some people feel they have no obligations to anyone, as you'll see in the next chapter.

There are certain things you can't say to the media while you are playing in the NBA. But there's one story I always wanted to tell ... about Larry Bird. Unfortunately Bird is one of the superstars who carries the NBA. So he gets preferential treatment from everybody, including the fans, the press, and the officials.

10
THE GOOSE THAT LAID THE GOLDEN EGG IS SICK—
AND I DON'T FEEL SO GOOD MYSELF

There are certain things that you can't say to the media about your teammates or opponents while you are playing in the NBA. You also can't say them about your coach, your owner, or the conditions under which you are playing. Because a player learns to stay out of the headlines for things he says or does off the court.

But there's one story I always wanted to tell . . . about Larry Bird. He is the most popular player in the NBA, although he still has a lot to learn—and I still feel Kareem Abdul-Jabbar is the greatest ever to play the game. Contrary to what you might think, I am not personal friends with many of the superstars, including Larry Bird, who is considerably younger than I.

One night Bird did something to embarrass me, something that just underscores the lack of feeling that some younger players apparently have toward the fans and the game. Many young stars are babied, and when the cheering stops, they can't function in the real world.

A teenage daughter of a friend of mine from Kentucky idolized Larry Bird. I told my friend I'd take her down to McNichols Sports Arena when the Celtics came to Denver so that she could meet him. I knew it was going to be a bit difficult, since the Celtics only played in Denver once every season. And I had never really had any contact with Bird, so I didn't really know what to expect.

I sent word to the locker room that I'd like to meet Bird in the hallway after the game. When he came out, I introduced the young girl to him. Naturally, she wanted his autograph. Being a player, I realized how demanding the fans can be, so I tried to be discreet about it. Well, he acted like the whole thing was a royal pain, as if I were overstepping my boundaries. I've never seen Julius or Kareem act that way. He didn't say a word, just signed the program, nodded, and took off.

Ordinarily, when another player asks a favor, you try to make the guy feel big, not like a jerk. I always ask, while I'm signing the program "How's the weather back in Kentucky?" Or Phoenix. Or Washington, DC. Wherever. Bird was a mute. I don't think I'll ever forgive him for that.

That just points up the larger problem today with the "give-me-mine" mentality of athletes. It's an illness brought about by huge salaries and long-term contracts. There is more to basketball than what you produce on the court, even for the superstars. You have to give something back. I hope that Larry Bird learns that someday.

Unfortunately, Bird is one of the superstars who carries the NBA. He has been pampered because the NBA needs Larry Bird like the Democrats need presidential fodder. He gets preferential treatment from everybody, including the fans, the press, and the officials.

Athletes and sports franchises, however, must endure the same problems as any other groups—families, businesses, civic clubs, whatever. Just because a guy wears a jock doesn't mean he is immune to the problems of society. There are squabbles, fist fights, petty jealousies, spoiled brats, egomaniacs, alcoholics, drug addicts, gamblers, thieves, womanizers, and homosexuals. Basketball is unique, however, in the amount of pressure brought to bear on the athlete. It's incredible.

The 82-game schedule brings out the worst in everybody.

Life is a series of one-nighters. You take a kid right out of college, give him a fistful of money, put him in a strange environment where he has nothing but idle time and lonely hotel rooms, and you are lighting the fuse of a powder keg.

Not only that, but the 82-game schedule dilutes the product substantially. I don't care if you're Larry Bird or Rory Sparrow, there is no way you can play 82 regular-season games over a five-and-a-half month period and be able to give each game your all. You might be giving it all that you have left, but what you have left isn't ready-for-prime-time basketball.

This is something that the public perceives, but apparently NBA owners don't. I've always thought if teams weren't playing three or four times a week, each game would mean more, people would be more interested in the outcome, and attendance figures would be at least as high, if not higher. Plus owners would get a better performance from their players while putting them through less wear and tear. In other words, if the quantity of games went down, the quality of and the demand for those games would go up.

Maybe what the NBA needs is a basketball-game shortage, like the American gas shortage of 1974.

That basic premise of supply and demand, which we all learn in first-year high school economics, has apparently eluded the NBA owners completely. They argue that, if you reduce the schedule by 20 games, the 31 home games remaining couldn't make as much money even if they drew 30 percent more fans. I guess it has to do with revenues from concessions, parking, etc., but I say that by having 41 home games the fans just pick and choose certain games without having to buy season tickets. They know Boston and Philadelphia only come to places like Denver once a year, so why bother buying a season-ticket package that includes Cleveland, Indianapolis, and Golden State?

Which brings up another problem of the NBA: the dichotomy between the haves and the have-nots. If you're honest, you know that only three teams have a chance at winning the NBA title: the Celtics, the Lakers, and the 76ers. And, now that they have Patrick Ewing, maybe you could include the Knicks. In the case of Ewing, the rich got richer again. The NBA lottery did nothing to improve the hopes of the fans in San Francisco, for instance.

So it's a vicious circle. The NBA cannibalizes itself. Fans don't come to the games because they don't get to see the contenders play enough. Owners don't make enough money to pay the high salaries, so they extend the schedule to 82 games, which is the reason the quality of play has fallen off. Thus we have the state of affairs that currently exists.

Despite my criticism of the NBA, I am still bullish on it. I think the new commissioner, David Stern, is aware of what's going on and will deal with the problems. He has already dealt with a number of them, including the drug problem. Hopefully, the long schedule is another one that will be addressed soon, although as long as the fans tolerate those 30- and 40-point blowouts, the owners are going to get in every last regular-season game they can. Which is the reason fans always tell me: "I don't start watching the NBA until the playoffs." Or, "It doesn't matter what happens in the game until the last two minutes." Pretty soon it's going to reach the point where fans stop coming to the arenas and start switching off their TV sets.

I think that's already happening in other sports, like football's NFL and USFL. The Cowboys no longer sell out in Dallas, which means not only aren't they "America's Team," they aren't even Dallas's team. Oddly enough, through sound marketing strategy, the Dallas Mavericks have developed a strong season-ticket base and the NBA is thriving in Dallas. The Mavericks now have the model program for marketing, and it's being studied all over the NBA.

The whole salary structure begins and ends with an assessment of what the market will bear. And how much an NBA player is worth. Certainly, when it reaches today's dimensions, when the average salary is more than $300,000, you must question it in earnest. I suppose you can take both sides of that argument:

Side one: Should a pro athlete make five times the amount of money that the president of the United States is making, more than the chairman of a big corporation?

Side two: Should an entertainer, like Bruce Springsteen, make more money from one concert than some of the best athletes in the world make for a whole season?

So you see, in theory at least, it's fair market value. I'm not going to be hypocritical, because I've benefited from the skyrocketing salaries, although not as much as most. I'm like Goose Gossage, who signed a huge contract as a free agent with the San Diego Padres. Goose said, "I'd pitch for $30,000 a year if that was the going rate for top relief pitchers. But if they're going to pay a million dollars, I want what the top guys are making."

What throws a monkey wrench into the "fair market value" theory are people like George Steinbrenner of the Yankees and Ted Stepien, the former owner of the Cavaliers. I'm not saying the two men are just alike, because obviously, Steinbrenner is a much shrewder businessman and more successful owner. Stepien had a brief fling with the Cavs, giving away the store to second-rate players and almost putting the city of Cleveland out of the basketball business. But both Steinbrenner and Stepien were willing to pay more than fair market value for players, and that threw the scale out of whack. The USFL did the same thing for a while to the football market, although the NFL was smart enough not to follow the trend. That's why there were so many hard-line negotiations, why players such as the Dolphins' Dan Marino and the Rams' Eric Dickerson were holding out.

I think pro basketball was ahead of other pro sports. We were the first with the big salaries—David Thompson's $800,000 a year for example—and the first with salary caps, and we'll probably begin to see the same thing happen to football and baseball eventually.

The NBA has begun to get its house in order. The players have never had a strike. The league has taken a stronger position on drugs, and it has attended to the problem of teams going in the tank to get high draft choices. I've got a reason to think that David Stern will continue his aggressive stance on improvement of the NBA.

It boils down to one thing: the product that goes out there on the floor. And, ultimately, the fans will have to be the judge of that.

Sometimes I think that owners of pro sports teams need to be saved from themselves. Greed seems to haunt them. For instance, the USFL started with the idea of limiting salaries, but that lasted only until some owner coveted a player and decided, "To hell with the rules. Think what the other members of my golf foursome will say on Saturday when I tell them I've just signed John Doe of State U."

For the most part, these are men who have been very successful in their respective fields—real estate, oil, food franchising, advertising, etc. They made a lot of money making astute decisions. Nobody every heard of them until they bought a pro sports franchise. Then everybody knows who they are and they start making horrible decisions, just because they like seeing their name in the papers everyday. They don't run their sports franchises with the same business acumen they exercise in their other line of work. It's amazing, isn't it?

For instance, I wonder if Dr. Jerry Buss, owner of the Lakers, didn't fall into that trap of putting "pride of ownership" before a good sound business decision in the case of Magic Johnson, who supposedly will get more than $2 million a year for the rest of his career. I mean, is *anybody* worth that kind of money for *anything*? Magic didn't cure cancer or achieve peace in the Middle East; he's just a great basketball player—and, granted, he's great. I don't begrudge him a nickel.

Despite the few differences of opinions I might have had with Red McCombs, who recently sold the Nugget franchise to Sidney Shlenker of Houston, I must compliment him on the way he ran the Nuggets. From what I'm able to discern from other sources, Red bought the Nuggets in 1982 for a song, maybe as low as $4 million. (Granted, it was a fire sale, because the Nuggets had cash-flow problems and had accrued a large debt, not the least of which was from financing the indemnity the ABA had to pay for merging with the NBA. And, I'm told, Red sold the Nuggets for $20 million.

If you had any other piece of property and could turn a profit

like that over a period of three years, they would write you up
in *Fortune* magazine. Yet people questioned why Red would
want to sell the Nuggets. Unlike some of the other owners, Red
seemed to be capable of differentiating between hobbies and
businesses. If everybody else approached ownership of sports
franchises as Red did, the leagues would be in a lot better
shape today. Unfortunately, to most money men, it's a lot more
impressive to go to a cocktail party and say, "I own the Denver
Nuggets" than it is to say, "I just sold the Denver Nuggets and
made $16 million."

Red and I started out under difficult circumstances, but the
more I got to know him, the more I understood and respected
him. I was a free agent when he bought the club, and I had
good leverage, because he needed me a lot more than I needed
pro basketball. So I was able to get what I wanted, which was
$600,000 a year, plus perks. To Red's credit, he never let
personalities get into the negotiations.

(But this man who paid me 600 grand a year to play basketball showed he wasn't all business when he bought me a truck
painted "Kentucky Blue" which was presented to me the night
I retired. He didn't really have to buy me a truck, although, as
it turns out, he could well afford it. And I appreciated it a great
deal.)

Owners in the NBA ought to know better, but they insist on
tying up players to these long-term, multi-year contracts. It
seems obvious that the high salaries in themselves might not be
so bad, but the long-term contracts are not conducive to good
performance; they actually kill incentive and turn the players
into fat cats. No matter how badly they play, they're still getting
a half-million bucks, or whatever, a year. This garbage line that
we always hear from athletes after they've signed long-term
deals is really a crock: "Well, I feel better now because the
future of my family is secure." Baloney. Nobody's future is
secure if the league goes out of business.

I think that during the old days of baseball, when players
signed one-year contracts, you got more honest performances.
In the off-season, the general manager sent you a contract in

the mail. If you hit .320, had a great year coming out of the bullpen, or won 20 games, you got a raise. If you had a bad year, your salary was lower. Whichever way, the return on performance was immediate. I think the players were hungrier because they had incentive to play well.

Salaries aren't the only element in which superstars have the upper hand. They also get the edge when it comes to officiating. I've already expressed myself on the matter of officials, but there is at least one dilemma for the referees that has no easy solution: the double standard for superstars. Nobody talks about it publicly, but it's there.

Everybody realizes superstars are the bread-and-butter performers in the NBA. People who pay $20 a ticket don't want to see a Julius Erving or Larry Bird or Kareem Abdul-Jabbar sitting on the bench in foul trouble. So, as a result, the superstars get preferential treatment; allowances are made for certain aspects of their game.

Maybe it's okay to give them special consideration on certain plays. If Dr. J goes up on a jam and takes an extra step on his takeoff, he's probably not going to get called for walking. If Larry Bird drives the baseline and throws an elbow just before he gets off a 20-footer, maybe he gets away with it. It's not necessarily a conscious decision on the part of the officials. It sort of comes with the territory. Like if Johnny Carson walks into your restaurant, he doesn't have to go to the end of the line; he gets a table right away.

Sometimes it's more the style of the player than it is his stature. I think they give an extra step to Mark Aguirre of the Mavericks. Moses Malone of the Sixers is probably allowed to push off more than most players because he's known to be very physical. When he played for the Bullets, Wes Unseld got a reputation for being able to block out and was a great rebounder, and it got to the point where, if you tried to set up at the low post, he would put two hands in your lower back and give you a shove. There was never a call, because he was known as a good inside player. And, because he's such a good free-throw shooter, Adrian Dantley of Utah is adept at drawing fouls. Every time an opponent gets close to him, there's a whistle. If they touch him under the basket while he's shooting, it's automatically two free throws.

So I think the superstars get the reputations for certain parts of their game, and those reputations result in them getting preferential treatment.

And it can work the other way, too. Danny Schayes of the Nuggets is known for getting quick fouls and turnovers as soon as he comes off the bench, and I swear, it's almost as if they're waiting for him to make a mistake and—*TWEET!*—Danny gets nailed for something.

I don't think I ever got away with much of anything. Maybe it was because I was hard on the officials when I first came into the ABA. When I was younger, I was much more verbal and would get more technical fouls. The first year, the fine was only $25 per technical, so I got a bundle of them. But, as I got more mature and in better standing with the officials, as the technicals got more expensive, and as Cheri got on my case harder, they became less and less frequent.

Even though I'm out of it, basketball is still my game. And I'm a fan like everybody else. As I've said, my favorite player of all time is Kareem Abdul-Jabbar. That's why I've devoted most of this next chapter to the greatest player in the history of the NBA.

"

When God made the prototype of the perfect basket-ball player, it seems unfair that he put all the parts in one body. Kareem's even got straight front teeth. His own. That really frosts me.

"

11
THERE'S KAREEM, AND THEN THERE'S THE REST OF THE KROP

Contrary to those who think of me as Methuselah, I did not hand Dr. Naismith the hammer when he tacked up the peach basket, so I haven't seen everybody who ever wore a jock in the NBA. But it would be difficult, if not impossible, to imagine anybody ever playing better than Number 33 of the Lakers. Before I get into why he's the best, let me even the score with Kareem Abdul-Jabbar:

Kareem, you're a kareep!

There, now I feel better, because I've been owing the Big Sky-Hooker that one ever since the 1977 NBA All-Star Game in Milwaukee, when he pulled a cheap, high schoolish, hot-dog stunt to deflect the fans' anger. I wound up with the brunt of that anger directed at me instead. This may sound a bit harsh about a guy I'm canonizing in print, but I've been steaming about this, itching to get even, for more than eight years.

Nineteen seventy-seven was the year that Denver basketball fans stuffed the NBA All-Star ballot boxes to get recognition for their favorite players. The Nuggets had just gotten into the NBA and some over-zealous but well-meaning fans stayed up around the clock to mark ballots so that David Thompson, Bobby Jones, and I would make the starting lineup. They did, and we did. I had no part in the deal, which the fans thought was a brilliant idea, but I ultimately suffered the consequences of it.

Writers and fans in other cities got on my case about it. Every city I went to, the press would ask me, "Do you think you deserve to be starting ahead of Bill Walton and Kareem Abdul-Jabbar?" That's like somebody asking, "Do you think you're overpaid for a big white stiff who can't jump?" I knew I wasn't better than them, but I was having a good year and it wasn't as though I didn't deserve to be on the All-Star team. So I wasn't embarrassed by being selected, even if I didn't deserve to start. I wasn't the guy who stuffed the ballot box; as I told the press, "I didn't cast one single vote."

It hurt my pride because I wasn't exactly a second-rate player, but I began to feel like a leper. The heat from the L.A. press was really scorching my butt. So, the final game before the All-Star break, we played the Lakers and I scored 36 points. That was a little exclamation point from me for the L.A. folks, to let them know that, even though Kareem was the best, I wasn't exactly chopped liver.

A few nights before at Portland, I was roundly booed, both when I was introduced in the Nugget starting lineup and again during the game. But that was nothing compared to what was awaiting me at the All-Star game in Milwaukee—thanks mostly to Kareem's theatrics.

If anybody was going to be a villain in Milwaukee, you'd certainly think it would have been Kareem. He's the ex-Buck who deserted the fans, saying, "This place stinks" and bailing out for Los Angeles. He hadn't been back there much since he was traded to the Lakers after the 1974–75 season, so they should have been waiting in the bushes for him. Yet, somehow I was the villain and Kareem the hero. The people of Milwaukee were proud to be hosting an All-Star game and they apparently felt cheated that they were stuck with Dan Issel in the starting lineup.

Since he wasn't starting, Kareem was introduced ahead of me. Well, he just happened to forget his Laker warmups, but he did manage to remember his old Milwaukee Buck warmup jacket, which he came trotting out in. Talk about orchestrating a standing ovation—you'd have thought he had never left Milwaukee. The place went crazy.

You can imagine the reception they then gave me. I was humiliated. On what should have been a glorious night, my one and only chance to play in an NBA All-Star game, I wanted to run and hide. Looking back on it, I should have. I played 10 minutes and didn't score a point.

Kareem, who had the crowd in the palm of his hand, played 23 minutes and scored 21.

And the bad guy ran off with their hearts. That speaks pretty well of his knowledge about mob psychology: he turned a potentially hostile crowd into a bunch of allies. They were ready to lynch me for something I hadn't even done. Yet they forgave him for spitting in their faces.

That's about the only fault I can find with Kareem, because in my book—and I guess this *is* my book—he's the best that ever played the game.

In *his* book, *Giant Steps,* Kareem says that Oscar Robertson was the best all-round player he ever saw and called him "Thomas Edison," because Robertson was so inventive on the court. If Oscar was Thomas Edison, then Kareem is Albert Einstein, because he is equally as brilliant.

He floats like a butterfly and dunks like a donut.

He dominates a basketball court like Loni Anderson in a Phyllis Diller lookalike contest.

He has the stature of a giant redwood tree, the grace of a swan, the heart of a lion, and the instincts of a hawk.

Almost anytime he wants to, he can go to the hoop and score. Which is why he's the NBA's all-time leader in points. Anyway you want to slice it, he comes up the best.

Six times the NBA's Most Valuable Player. Fourteen NBA All-Star appearances (he declined once). Played as many seasons, 16, as anybody in history.

If you want to talk stats, he's got those: he averaged nearly 28 points a game for his career, playoffs, and regular season, totaling 37,812 combined points.

If you want to talk championships, he's won all kinds, starting at Power Memorial High School in New York City. Also, three NCAA titles at UCLA along with being named Most Outstanding

Player in all three tournaments and four NBA championships, one with Milwaukee, three with the Lakers.

There may never be another basketball player as good as Kareem Abdul-Jabbar. I consider it an honor and a privilege to have been in the same box score with him.

Even at age 38, he had a remarkable 1984–85 season as the Lakers won another title, averaging 22 points and nine rebounds. That's the mark of a great player, when he's not only great, but great for a long time. Consistency and durability: when you hold his career up to the light, those are the things that come shining through.

They could take Kareem to a taxidermist, stuff him, and stick him out on the court and he'd be worth 10 points to the Lakers just because he was standing there. Everybody is in awe of him, including his foes and his teammates. When the Lakers need a rebound, they look to Kareem. When the Lakers need a bucket, they look to Kareem. When the Lakers need leadership, they look to Kareem.

And he seldom disappoints.

It may be difficult for a layman to appreciate the rare combination of size, speed, skill, and strength—not to mention smarts—that he has in that one body. He has remarkable touch on the ball, quick feet, and graceful moves.

When God made the prototype of the perfect basketball player, it seems unfair that He put all the parts in one body. Kareem's even got straight front teeth. His own. That really frosts me.

The first time I ever saw Kareem, then known as Lew Alcindor, was when I was a freshman at the University of Kentucky in the spring of 1967, when the NCAA championships were held in Lexington. Since Kentucky went 13–13 that season, obviously we weren't playing in the Final Four. Besides, freshmen weren't eligible, anyway. So I was a ballboy in the Final Four, which is the closest I ever came to actually being in the tournament.

I sat right under the goal and gawked at the tall, giraffelike center for UCLA with the ballet moves, the likes of which this country boy had never seen. I couldn't take my eyes off him. Being 6'9" and having to fight awkwardness and clumsiness all my life, I was amazed to see how graceful a big man could be. He was a remarkable force, dominating both ends of the floor as no college player had ever dominated it before. He was incredible. And he was only a sophomore.

It was nine years before I ever had the privilege of playing against him. I had gone to the Colonels in the ABA; he had gone to Milwaukee in the NBA. So, it wasn't until 1976, when the Nuggets joined the NBA, that I found out what it was like going head-to-head with the greatest.

Because my style was so different from his and I played the pivot more like a high post, I actually fared pretty well against him over the years. The first few years I played against him, he would never come out and guard me, so when my jump shot was going down, I scored a bit. It is comforting to know that when you are going up against a guy like Kareem—a guy who keeps you from taking the ball to the basket—you can shoot jump shots without him bothering you. That lasted for a while. But in later years he started coming out to guard me and it got increasingly difficult to get off those jump shots.

One thing I learned: don't ever try to get physical with Kareem. He's a finesse player and he doesn't like the contact, but he's capable of banging when he wants to bang. I found out that it's better to let a sleeping Kareem lie, because if he decides to come at you he's going to have the upper hand. So I tried to fight finesse with finesse, letting him take his sky-hook, but making him take a step away from the basket instead of toward it. When he made his move, I would step in and try to force him away from the hoop. Sometimes it worked, sometimes it didn't but at least on most nights I was able to avoid being embarrassed.

I certainly don't want to imply I was ever in control on those encounters, because I wasn't. But on a few occasions I was able to keep it even, and that was a great victory for me.

I tried never to get him riled up. Once, years ago, when we first played against each other, I was having a particularly hot night from the outside. He jumped out to guard me, I went around him and made the fatal mistake of dunking the ball. The next three trips down the court, he made me pay dearly— he dunked right in my face. I got the message: don't ever embarrass him again. I played just as hard as ever, but I was a little more discreet about my style. You don't tug on Superman's cape.

We never got a chance to socialize, to eat dinner together, or develop an off-court relationship, but I got to know him pretty well just from talking during the games, and having a laugh now and then. Sometimes when I would foul him and the officials would miss it, I'd say: "Hey, Kareem, I owe you one." We'd make fun of other players or talk about a good play by somebody. It was never, "So how are the kids?" or, "How do you like the new house?" or, "I've got a horse for you. Let's grab a beer after the game and I'll tell you about it." Just a little dialogue, mostly humorous, and I even got him to crack up a few times. Evidently he enjoyed it as much as I did, because in *Giant Steps* he talks about our conversations:

> "Some guys you just get a good feeling about. Dan Issel is a big white guy, solid player, competitor. I've never spent time with him socially, but I know him. And I like him. Dan is involved in the game, but he still has the awareness and perspective to stop and wonder at people doing marvelous things on the court, and he'll talk to me about it. At the foul line, or when we pass in the locker room hallway, we'll always have something to say, little things that are immediate and you're dealing with right there but that show some character. Wisecracks about the coaches or quick player critiques. One time I almost got him in trouble because I couldn't stop laughing at George McGinnis's foul shooting. I was standing at the lane grinning—George had a very weird shot-put motion, and when he looked like that and missed, it just struck me funny—and I got Issel going too. Dan didn't want to shake George's confidence, or get the coach down on his own back, so in between giggles he was trying to shut me up."

I never could shut him up. Or shut him down.

This is the amazing gift of sports—that two people from entirely different backgrounds, of different race and political persuasions, could come together and communicate as friends without ever interacting outside the arena. Dan Issel, a white boy from Batavia, Illinois, meets Kareem Abdul-Jabbar, a.k.a. Lew Alcindor, a black guy from Harlem.

There is a side of Kareem that the public doesn't know, that only a fellow competitor can sense. I feel strongly that he was somewhat misunderstood, especially by whites who resented him being the focal point of the UCLA dynasty, who resented his talent, who resented his religion and the fact that he changed his name. Of course, his detractors will say he brought much of that resentment on himself by being so militant and aloof. I was never around him during those times, but I can tell from competing against him that he is a decent human being, a warm and caring person, a man of considerable courage and spunk—and, most of all, a man with a great sense of humor. It's too bad that that sense of humor hasn't surfaced more often.

By reading his book, one comes to know more about his background, his struggles, his fears and insecurities. I found it both ironic and somewhat tragic that he eventually parted ways with the idol of his youth, Wilt Chamberlain, because they were at opposite ends of the political spectrum. Wilt supported Richard Nixon and that ripped it with Kareem, who's a liberal Democrat. Yet I know Kareem still respected Chamberlain as a player, because Wilt was magnificent.

Both Chamberlain and Bill Russell were big men ahead of their time. I think if they had had to face the kind of competition day in and day out that Kareem faces, they would have found it far more difficult to be as effective as they were.

Kareem is an ancient warrior now, about ready to retire, but when he goes there will be a giant void in the game of pro basketball that may never again be filled. Maybe in time people will be able to understand how and why Kareem slammed the door on everybody early in his career. The demands on his life must have been a tremendous burden, and maybe John Wooden was correct in shielding the militant young black man from the outside world. There are too many hucksters, too many parasites, too many jock-sniffers out there who can betray a young college athlete. After having been through some of that on a much smaller scale, I can't imagine what it was like for him, but for me it was painful. Sometimes it's just easier to kick the door shut rather than face the next person

who walks in—whether it's an investor, media-person, pro-
ducer, fan, or just a guy who wants to shake hands.

Perhaps one day, when his basketball career is over, we can
break bread together and relive some old war stories. I'd love
to have dinner with him, talk about this and that, and get to
know him better. I'd sure love the chance to tell him that on
Dan Issel's All-Time Greatest Team, he'd be number one on the
roster.

Picking an All-Time Greatest Team of five players may be an
impossible task, for I never saw some of them play and others
I saw play but not in their primes. It's obvious though, who the
center on my All-Time Greatest Team would be: Kareem would
be my captain.

Right behind Abdul-Jabbar is the Doc, Julius Erving—part
acrobat, part dancer, part juggler, all basketball player and the
number-two all-time scorer, when you add his 11,662 ABA
points with his 16,019 NBA points—which they will have to do
someday.

Julius is still a great player because he's changed his style to
adapt over the years. But I've seen Doc do things that nobody
in the NBA has ever seen. He could make the hair on the back
of your neck stand up. Back in the early seventies when he
played with the ABA's Virginia Squires and the New York Nets,
Doctor J played a game with which we in this universe are
unfamiliar.

In his hands with those long spindly fingers, the basketball
was helpless. It looked like a volley ball. He had jets on his
sneakers and when he came off the floor he had to radio the
control tower to avoid near-misses with other aircraft. He was
a black Peter Pan in an Afro flying solo over our heads.
Sometimes I would just stand there and stare in amazement.
Where some people needed an alley to drive through, he would
just hover up there and create his own air corridor. He would
dunk on and over and around people.

People still talk about the vertical leap he made at halftime of
the 1976 ABA All-Star Game in the slam-dunk contest at
Denver. I swear that he took off before he reached the foul line
and never touched wood until he had dunked. Naturally, he

won the contest. He repeated that move at the 1984 All-Star Game in Denver but didn't fly quite as far and didn't win the slam-dunk contest that year. That's okay, because Doc had nothing left to prove. If Oscar Robertson was Thomas Edison and Kareem Abdul-Jabbar is Albert Einstein, then Julius Erving is a combination of Chuck Yeager, the pilot, and Doug Henning, the magician.

No matter what Julius did with the basketball, it looked planned. But I'm convinced that when he left the ground, he had no preconceived notion of what he was going to do. If they gave points for creativity, he'd retire the trophy. He's still a great player, but a much smarter one who has altered his style to fit his strengths. And to think they used to say you couldn't win the championship with a guy like Erving. I wonder what brilliant coach or sportswriter thought that one up.

There is one more outstanding characteristic of Julius Erving. He reeks with class as a person. When his playing days are over, the NBA ought to hire him as an ambassador of basketball. Hell, he might be Commissioner someday. I know of no man as fine as Doc to go around the country and promote basketball.

Another guy of that era whose skills were equal to Doc's was George McGinnis, but George doesn't qualify for my All-Time Greatest Team because his career didn't last nearly as long. George always depended on his raw talent, and when that started to erode he didn't have any kind of game left, so he wasn't able to achieve any longevity.

So, Kareem, Julius . . . and the other member of my front line would have to be Larry Bird. Although I didn't get a chance to play against him that much, I've seen enough to know that he's one of the best. He is the complete opposite of Doc and Kareem because he doesn't have the great physical tools, but he's got an innate sense of where everything is on the basketball court. He sees all the players at all times, and knows where the ball is at all times, where it's going to be, and how to get to it via the shortest route. He loves the game and playing it seems to come very easily to him. Bird might be the best all-round player in the game and he's going to have many great seasons. And he may only be reaching his peak now.

Already, in just six short years, Bird has been on two championship clubs, named MVP of the playoffs, on the All-Star Game every year, and named to the All-NBA Team six out of six times. His mastery of the game is remarkable and I admire the passion with which he plays. He may not be as pretty or as creative as others in the NBA, but he is incredibly effective.

Trying to pick my All-Time Greatest Team's guards, I get into trouble. It's hard for me to imagine any guards ever being better than Oscar Robertson and Jerry West. I never played with them; I saw them play a little on TV while I was in the ABA and they were in the NBA, but both of them retired in the early seventies while I was still with the Colonels. Oscar, as Kareem said, could do it all, and Kareem should know, because they were teammates at Milwaukee. People talk about Magic Johnson's "triple double stat" (points, assists, and rebounds), which we all sort of think was a creation of Magic's. I didn't know until I read in Kareem's book that Oscar's average—*average*—was nearly a triple double for his entire career: 26 points, 10 assists, and eight rebounds for more than 1,000 regular-season games.

So, I have to go with Oscar at one guard and West at the other for my team. Jerry was a pure shooter with a slick outside jumper, a 12-time All-Star who still holds the record for the highest NBA playoff scoring average—29.1 in 153 games. Jerry shot over 47 percent for his career and considering that most of those shots came from outside, that's quite a feat.

Could be that Magic will wind up surpassing both West and Robertson. We tend to forget that Magic is still a young pup— just 26 going into his seventh NBA season in 1985. He could be whatever he wants to be in the game of basketball—scorer, rebounder, defender, passer, ball-handler. And his stats won't wind up reflecting his superb talent because he always puts teamwork ahead of personal bests, and has never put a high premium on scoring. He has already broken the playoff record for career assists and been on three NBA championship teams.

If I could have more than five players, Magic would be on my All-Time Greatest Team. I'd also like to have David Thompson—that is, the younger version that I played with the first three years in Denver. David was on his way to becoming something special, when he first got to the NBA: he could jump and hang in the air longer than anybody I ever saw. If longevity wasn't a criterion, David Thompson would be on my squad.

Several remarkably talented young players in the NBA now impress me greatly. After just one year, it's clear that Michael Jordan of the Chicago Bulls has "superstar" written all over him. Jordan is the first player to come along in a while who I would put in a category with Julius Erving or David Thompson. The best thing about Jordan is that he seems to have his head screwed on right. Coach Dean Smith of North Carolina has a reputation for turning out that kind of player. To have the success that Jordan has already had after only one season in the NBA, and to have handled it with such maturity, he's shown that he has a bright future in the NBA.

It takes longer for the big men to come around in the NBA than it does the smaller, gifted people, so that's why the fans were up in arms about the Trail Blazers passing over Jordan in favor of the taller Sam Bowie. It is going to take another year or two for Bowie, but don't count him out. He's going to be a star in the league, too.

Ralph Sampson of Houston is going to be a great player just because of his enormous physical stature and skills. He really started to come on in 1985, but you'd think a 7'4" player would be able to come underneath the basket and dunk. It puzzles me that Ralph seldom does that. But he has amazing touch and ball-handling skills, and can play just about any position on the court.

Akeem Olajuwon of Houston is going to take a while. He has a longer way to go, because he's only been playing basketball for five or six years, so the jury is still out on him. If he's willing to work hard at it, he's got a chance to be among the best.

This is in no way a compendium of all the great players: I'm simply attempting to name my top five, although I've had to throw in a few stragglers. That's not to say I'd leave out people like Bill Russell, Wilt Chamberlain, Pete Maravich, Bob Petit, Earl Monroe, Bob Cousy, John Havlicek, Elgin Baylor, George Gervin, Bill Walton, Artis Gilmore, Kiki Vandeweghe, Moses Malone, or Alex English.

But I did—this time.

"

LEAST FAVORITE ARENA: Boston Garden—Smells like a circus. Terrible playing surface. No air conditioning. Plus you have to play the Celtics.

"

12
DAN ISSEL'S FIVE-STAR RATING GUIDE
AND OTHER ALL-TIME NONSENSE

This rating guide isn't going to threaten the sales of the *Michelin Guide*, but after 15 years of traveling the country and playing pro basketball, I've gathered all this valuable research, and the least I can do is pass it on for your edification.

The truth is that I've collected all this meaningless drivel and I've got to find a place to dump it, so this is as good a place as any. If, perchance, any of this happens to be interesting or significant to you, it's purely coincidental.

★ ★ ★ ★ ★

I'm confining the travelogue portion of this guide to NBA cities because it's been a while since I've toured the ABA route and visited places like Greensboro, North Carolina.

The reader should understand, too, that my judgment is somewhat warped. I see things from a different perspective, and I'm jaded by my lack of perception. When I'm rating cities, such things as museums and theaters don't matter to me. Unless the city has a racetrack, it doesn't qualify for the Issel Five-Star Award.

Restaurants? They sometimes help but aren't vital. On the road, I ate almost all my meals in my room, so what was important to me was a hotel's room service. If I didn't go to a racetrack, I would room-service it and watch TV. I was a great reader and TV watcher on the road. A lot of players will take in the sights, go shopping, hit bars, or go to nice restaurants.

Basically, I'm fairly boring. So this rating guide will reflect that narrow point of view. Well, here goes:

DAN ISSEL'S FIVE-STAR CITIES

1. **Los Angeles**—A horse-playing basketball player's paradise, with Hollywood Park situated right across the street from The Forum, and Santa Anita over in Arcadia.
2. **New York**—The room service is usually good and one is never far away from Belmont Park or Aqueduct.
3. **Phoenix**—The warm sun on one's back feels great when there's a foot of snow in Denver. My last two years, I had horses running there that spent the winters at Turf's Paradise.
4. **Chicago**—Because my family is there. And because Arlington Park and Sportsman's Park are, too.
5. **Seattle and San Francisco**—Such pretty places. The race tracks are average, but both have such fine food that occasionally I even skipped room service there.

LEAST FAVORITE: **Milwaukee**—and I don't need to tell you why.

RUNNERUP: **Baltimore**—if it were in the NBA.

Comment: I don't care what Rand McNally said in its nation-wide rating of the best cities, Pittsburgh wouldn't make my top 50. I'd rate it just barely ahead of Baltimore, and you already know how I feel about Baltimore.

DAN ISSEL'S FIVE-STAR ARENAS

I don't like any of the arenas that were made for football or baseball, like the Kingdome, the Silverdome, or the Superdome, so they don't qualify.

1. **Madison Square Garden, New York**—Most famous in the country. The fans and the media know the game. Fans may be a bit rowdy, but they appreciate excellence and applaud it. In Portland, they cheer the home team no matter what and boo the opposition. That's bush. In New York, when the Knicks stink, the fans let them know.
2. **The Forum, Los Angeles**—Even though the building is starting to age, it has a certain elegance. I had some pretty decent games there, and my last one will always be special.
3. **Reunion Arena, Dallas**—Brand new facility, enthusiastic crowd. And we stayed right across the street.
4. **Salt Palace, Utah**—They booed me there, but Coach Rupp always said that was a compliment. I have a soft spot in my heart for the place because of all the ABA games I played there. And any place where Frank Layden coaches has to be okay.
5. **Market Square, Indiana**—I admit that it's special to me because the Colonels played there in the 1975 ABA title series.

LEAST FAVORITE: **Boston Garden**—Smells like a circus. Terrible playing surface. No air conditioning. And it's falling apart. Plus you have to play the Celtics.

ROOM SERVICE

My order was always the same: hamburger, French fries, salad, and iced tea. The criteria for this honor are:

- It must be 24-hour service, because we're usually scrambling late at night for something to eat.
- Condiments: there must be salt, pepper, sugar, cream, water, crackers, etc., to go with the food.
- The time between when the order is placed and the food's arrival must not be more than 20 minutes, and the food must be kept hot.

1. **Westin Hotel, Seattle**—Simply the best, hands down. Sometimes I was torn between this city's outstanding restaurants and this country's best room service.
2. **Hilton, Los Angeles**—Good menu, courteous waiters.
3. **Hyatt-Regency, Dallas**
4. **Hyatt, Oakland**—A guy named Danny has been bringing me room service there for five years, and he knows exactly how I like everything. The hotel is average, but Danny brings it up to a contender.
5. **Marriot, Salt Lake City**

★ ★ ★ ★ ★

Enough trappings. Now for the basketball stuff.

DAN ISSEL'S FIVE-STAR OFFICIALS
. . . WELL, OKAY,
AT LEAST TWO-STAR OFFICIALS

It's difficult to come up with five of them. It's also impossible to give any of them five stars. My first choice gets four and a half.

1. **Earl Strom**—As I've said, he has a sense of humor, and he'll talk to players and admit it if he's wrong.
2. **Darrell Garretson**
3. **John Vanak**
4. **Jack Madden**
5. **Jess Kersey**

WORST: **Joey Crawford**

DAN ISSEL'S
FIVE-STAR NBA COACHES

I'm at a handicap here, because so many great coaches weren't contemporaries of mine. Red Auerbach, for instance. He's obviously one of the best, having won nine championships with the Celtics and boasting the best winning percentage in the league's history (66 percent).

So, in general, this list is for modern-day, active NBA coaches. Well, I can't rate them, but I can name the best:

- **Doug Moe,** Denver Nuggets—I've devoted a whole chapter to Doug, but let me say one more thing about him. If you have the best talent in the NBA and win 60 games on the way to the title, that doesn't necessarily mean you are the best coach. A good coach is one who gets more out of that team than anybody has a right to expect. Doug gets far more than anybody has a right to out of the Nuggets.

- **Dick Motta,** Dallas Mavericks—Especially because of his eye for talent, his developmental program, and the way he's built Dallas into a contender. There were some names in the expansion draft that could have given the Mavs instant credibility, but Motta was wise to build through the draft; stockpiling the draft choices and building the club as quickly as he did was sheer genius on Motta's part. . . . Everybody says Dallas is just a big man away from a division title. Since the Mavs got Mark Acres (the seven-footer from Oral Roberts), Uwe Blab (the 7'2" German from Indiana), and Detlef Schrempf (the 6'9" German from Washington), maybe they are on their way.

- **Jack Ramsay,** Portland Trail Blazers—A scholar of the game, he takes it seriously, which is why he is nicknamed "the Professor." He's a real teacher and gets right down to basics. I like to think of basketball as more of a game than he does, but his method is proven; I don't especially like his style, but I admire the results he gets.

- **Don Nelson,** Milwaukee Bucks—A tough disciplinarian, he seems to motivate his players without lording over them. He's a player's type of coach and a guy I would have enjoyed playing for. Maybe I'll come out of retirement and play for him, but he'd have to move out of Milwaukee.
- **John MacLeod,** Phoenix, Suns—He has accomplished a great deal. He's never had a dominating center, but gets hustle and leadership from his players. He coaches in the style that's best for the talent, not necessarily the way he'd like to coach. John is a real achiever, and even though he doesn't have a handful of championship rings, he gets the best out of the team.
- **Pat Riley,** Los Angeles Lakers—Some people say that the Lakers have so much talent that all Pat has to do is make out the lineup card and roll the ball out on the floor. I don't agree. Pat has spent a lot of time and energy on that job, working to become a complete coach. One night, my business partner, Tom Gentry, and I invited Pat to join us for dinner after a Laker game. Pat said no, he'd have to go home and start looking at films for the next game. I think he has a particularly hard job, keeping all those egos in line. The results are speaking for themselves. I was impressed by the way he brought the Lakers back from that humiliating defeat in Boston in the 1983–84 championship series to win the title in 1985.

★ ★ ★ ★ ★

Now, on to more serious stuff, stuff that is the result of 15 years of closely studying the social interaction of the Homo sapien and the impact of the mores of our society on him. Stuff like . . .

DAN ISSEL'S ALL-FAT TEAM

Player	Team	Weight
Charles Barkley	76ers	260
Billy Paultz	Jazz	255
Dave Corzine	Bulls	260
Jeff Ruland	Bullets	245
Fat Lever (Honorary Captain)	Nuggets	170

Coach: Frankie Layden

At one time, before I lost about 20 pounds a couple of years ago, I might have qualified for the All-Fat Team myself. I figure if we ever got our fast break going, we could roll on forever.

DAN ISSEL'S ALL-FOREIGN BORN TEAM

Player	Team	Birthplace
Patrick Ewing	Knicks	Kingston, Jamaica
Dominique Wilkins	Hawks	Paris, France
Kiki Vandeweghe	Blazers	Weisbaden, Germany
Akeem Olajuwon	Rockets	Laos, Nigeria
James Donaldson	Clippers	Meachern, England

I thought seriously about having an All-German Born Team, with Kiki Vandeweghe, rookies Detlef Schrempf (Leverküsen) and Uwe Blab (Munich) of Dallas, and Scott Endelin of Indiana (Heidelberg), but we fell one starter short.

DAN ISSEL'S ALL-JOHNSON, ALL-GUARD TEAM

Player	Team	Position
Magic Johnson	Lakers	Guard
Eddie Johnson	Hawks	Guard
Dennis Johnson	Celtics	Guard
Vinnie Johnson	Pistons	Guard
Frank Johnson	Bullets	Guard

Coach: Phil Johnson, Kansas City

And, in case they needed a front line: Clarence Johnson of Chicago, Clemon Johnson of Philadelphia, and the two George Johnsons, one of Philadelphia and the other of New Jersey.

Naturally, they would play in Johnson City, Tennessee, in Johnson & Murphy sneakers on a floor cleaned with Johnson's wax. The only ice cream served would be Howard Johnson's. One more item: Gus Johnson, wrapped in Johnson & Johnson bandages, would make a comeback.

I've always been enamored of names. Middle names are about as useful as glass milk bottles: nice to have around as a remembrance but not very functional. So I made up two teams of the most unusual and absurd middle names:

DANIEL PAUL ISSEL'S ALL-MIDDLE NAME TEAM

FIRST UNIT

Name	Team
Michael Leroyall Evans	Nuggets
Pace Shewan Mannion	Jazz
Julius Winfield Erving	76ers
Lonnie Jewel Shelton	Cavaliers
Isiah Lord Thomas III (Captain)	Pistons

SECOND UNIT

Name	*Team*
Larry Donell Nance	Suns
Norm Ellard Nixon	Clippers
John MacBeth Paxson	Spurs
Richard Ryland Kelley	Jazz
Daniel LaDrew Vranes	Sonics

Coaches: Hubie Jude Brown, Knicks;
and William Fenton Russell, Celtics (retired)

Middle names aren't the only ones that go to waste. Sometimes a person's real name is more obscure than his nickname.

DAN "the Horse" ISSEL'S ALL-NICKNAME TEAM

Player	*Team*
Leonard Eugene "Truck" Robinson	Knicks
Carlton "Scooter" McCray	Sonics
Lafayette "Fat" Lever	Nuggets
Wayne Monte "Tree" Rollins	Hawks
Ernest Maurice "Kiki" Vandeweghe	Blazers

Coach: Lowell "Cotton" Fitzsimmons, Spurs

★   ★   ★   ★   ★

The following list required the most careful study and research. First I have to explain the term *big white stiff.* Not everybody can be a white stiff. Kareem, for instance, has no shot at this category; he jumps too high. A big white stiff is a guy who hardly gets off the floor when going for a rebound, who stands at least 6′10″, and averages fewer than 10 points a game. It helps a lot if he's awkward on his feet and shoots bricks.

DAN ISSEL'S
ALL-BIG WHITE STIFF TEAM

Player	Height	Team
Greg Kite	6'10"	Celtics
Steve Hayes	6'10"	Sixers
Scott Hastings	6'10"	Hawks
Randy Breur	7'3"	Bucks
Chuck Nevitt (Captain)	7'5"	Lakers

Traveling Squad: Chris Engler, 6'10", Bucks;
Fred Roberts, 6'10", Jazz; Rich Kelley, 7'0", Jazz

Missed by an Inch: Hank McDowell, 6'9", Houston

My enthusiastic choice for coach is Doug Moe of the Nuggets, even though he falls 5 inches under the requirement. I admit that it's a loaded choice, but Doug would be insulted to be left off this list.

★ ★ ★ ★ ★

I'm always amazed at the collegiate records of some players who bounce themselves around more than the ball, and at the oddly named colleges and universities that NBA players have attended:

DAN ISSEL'S ALL-ALUMNI TEAM

- **Lester Conner,** Warriors—Los Medanos College (Antioch, California); Chabot College (Hayward, California); and Oregon State.
- **Joe Cooper,** Sonics—Howard College (Big Spring, Texas); University of Tulsa; and University of Colorado.
- **Ricky Pierce,** Bucks—Walla Walla Community College (Washington)
- **Walker Russell,** Hawks—Oakland Community College (California); University of Houston; and Western Michigan.

- **Mitchell Wiggins,** Rockets (Captain)—Truett-McConnell College (Cleveland, Georgia); Clemson; and Florida State.
- *Traveling squad:* **Darryl Dawkins,** Nets—no college; **Moses Malone,** Sixers—no college. (Lowers the average.)
- *Coach:* **Chuck Daily,** Pistons—St. Bonaventure, Bloomsburg State College (Pennsylvania); and Penn State.

DAN ISSEL'S ALL-HOMETOWN TEAM

Hometown names are always good for a yuk or two. The more obscure, the better. These are among my favorites.

Player	Team	Town
Artis Gilmore	Spurs	Chipley, Florida
Robert Reed	Rockets	Shertz, Texas
Steve Stipanovich	Pacers	Creve Coeur, Minnesota
Joe Dumars	Pistons	Natchitoches, Louisiana
Calvin Duncan (Captain)	Cavaliers	Mouth of Wilson, Virginia

DAN ISSEL'S ALL-TRANSIENT TEAM

I know what it's like to be traded. Having played for three teams in my pro career, I'm aware that it's no fun. But there are some interesting cases in the NBA where some players have been swapped four, five, even six times for no apparent reasons.

The criterion for this honor: must have played with no fewer than four teams, or been cut more than three times.

- **Wayne Cooper,** Nuggets—Traded from Golden State to Utah, from Utah to Dallas, from Dallas to Portland, from Portland to Denver.
- **Brad Davis,** Mavericks—Waived by Los Angeles Lakers; signed by Indiana and waived; played in Western Basket-

ball Association and Continental Basketball Association; signed by Detroit and waived; signed by Dallas.

- **Charles Jones,** Bullets—Signed by Phoenix and waived; signed by Portland and waived; played in France, Italy, and on three different Continental Basketball Association teams; signed by San Antonio and waived; signed by Chicago and waived; signed by Washington.
- **Robert Smith,** Cavaliers (maybe)—Signed by Denver and waived; re-signed and traded to Utah, waived by Utah; signed by New Jersey and waived; signed by Cleveland and waived; signed by Kansas City and waived; signed by Milwaukee and waived; signed by San Diego and waived; signed by San Antonio and waived; signed by Cleveland and waived.
- **Steve Hayes,** Jazz (Captain)—Waived by New York; signed by Portland and waived; signed by Chicago and waived; signed by San Antonio to two 10-day contracts that expired; signed by Detroit and traded to Cleveland and waived; signed by Seattle and waived; signed by New Jersey and waived; signed by Sixers to 10-day contract that expired; signed by Utah.

★　★　★　★　★

I hope by now I've established that a healthy sense of humor is necessary for a professional athlete if he wants to keep his sanity. We players are constantly exposed to extreme highs and lows, one minute stressed out in the heat of battle, with all our pride and dignity at stake on the bounce of a ball; the next minute stretched out in our hotel rooms with nobody even to talk to about our problematic lives. I wish sometimes the public wouldn't take its heroes so seriously, would allow us a few foibles and indiscretions, and wouldn't put us on pedestals. It hurts both them and us too much when we fall off.

That's why humor helps. It punctures vanity and stabilizes egos. I hope my teammates and fellow players realize that when I poke fun at them I'm poking it at myself, too. For instance, in this next group of Five-Star Ratings, you will recognize a familiar name. All are former Nuggets.

DAN ISSEL'S WORST-DRESSED FORMER DENVER NUGGETS

Player	Current Team
Monte Towe	Retired
Rich Kelley	Jazz
Kiki Vandeweghe	Blazers
Bobby Jones	Sixers
Dan Issel (Captain)	Retired

Trainer: Bob "Chopper" Travaglini

While on the subject of the Nuggets, I should probably present my All-Bust Nugget team. The Nuggets are a classic example of how not to build through the draft. The only player on the 1984–85 Denver roster who was actually drafted was reserve guard Willie White. Mike Evans, one of two number-one picks in 1978, might count, but he was actually drafted for Kansas City and didn't join the Nuggets until 1983.

The Nugget drafts were legendary. We couldn't pick our grandmother out of Bruce Springsteen's band. Our general managers thought the draft was something they got when they opened the bedroom window. Here, then, in memory of our great recognition of college talent, are some of the Denver Nuggets' most notorious choices:

DAN ISSEL'S FIVE-STAR ALL-BUST NUGGETS

Player/College	Year	Pick
Tom LaGarde/North Carolina	1977	1st
Rod Griffin/Wake Forest	1978	1st
James Ray/Jacksonville	1980	1st
Rob Williams/Houston	1982	1st
Howard Carter/LSU	1983	2nd

It takes a real expert to pick out a hot dog: hot dogs aren't always readily recognizable by the general public, but a player knows a hot dog the instant he sees one. This is a very subjective list—and I'm not talking about the kind of hot dog you buy at the concession stand either.

DAN ISSEL'S FIVE-STAR NBA HOT DOGS

Player	Team	Variety
Reggie Theus	Kings	Oscar Meyer
Kevin McHale	Celtics	Two-Foot Long
Maurice Lucas	Lakers	A Real Dog
Bill Walton	Celtics	A Red Dog
Mark Aguirre	Mavericks	With Texas Chili

I don't want you to think I'm one of those negative types, like the young writers I've criticized. Lists can be positive, too, and just to prove that, here are some of my personal favorites.

DAN ISSEL'S FIVE-STAR SKY-WALKING LEAPERS

Criteria for this list: the best jumpers I ever played against. (I had an expert's view, standing flat-footed on the floor.)

Player	Team
David Thompson	Nuggets
Larry Nance	Suns
Dominique Wilkins	Hawks
Julius Erving	Sixers
Orlando Woolridge	Bulls

Then there are the horse lovers. This is my team of guys who own thoroughbreds and play in the NBA:

DAN ISSEL'S FIVE-STAR BASKETBALL-PLAYING HORSE OWNERS

Player	*Team*
Kiki Vandeweghe	Blazers
Kyle Macy	Suns
Jamaal Wilkes	Lakers
Don Buse	Kings
Rick Robey	Suns

And now for my favorite horses:

DAN ISSEL'S FIVE-STAR THOROUGHBREDS

1. Secretariat
2. Genuine Risk
3. John Henry
4. Ruffian
5. Seattle Slew

And, finally, no list of lists is ever complete without a list of favorite movies. Here's mine:

DAN ISSEL'S
FIVE-STAR MOVIES

1. *Stripes*
2. *Cool Hand Luke*
3. *Old Yeller*
4. *Gone with the Wind*
5. *Ten Commandments*

Looking over the lists I admit that some are a little biased. I noticed, for instance, that Kiki Vandeweghe's name shows up far too many times. But Kiki makes for such a good punching bag, I couldn't resist. No wonder he was always Doug Moe's favorite whipping boy.

Which reminds me—there's one more list:

DOUG MOE'S
FAVORITE PUNCHING BAGS

Criteria: Nugget players who have been hollered at the most by Doug in recent years.

1. Kiki Vandeweghe
2. Rob Williams
3. Dave Robisch
4. Danny Schayes
5. Wayne Cooper

★   ★   ★   ★   ★

One of the guys who always helped sooth players after Doug's screaming was Chopper, the trainer. Sometimes I think it was all an act, Doug screaming at them, Chopper taking them back to the training room and soothing them over—the "good cop, bad cop" routine. That's just one of the many things Chop does for the team. He is Mr. Everything to the Nuggets— trainer, traveling secretary, team shrink, confidant, father figure. And he was my best pal in Denver.

"I seriously considered writing Chop off as a dependent on last year's income taxes. One day, maybe I'll name a horse after him. I'll call it 'Free Lunch.'"

13
MY PAL CHOPPER
AND OTHER FRIENDS LEFT BEHIND IN THE ROCKIES

I don't know why I love Chopper like I do. He's gruff. He's full of hot air. He never picks up the check. He's always telling me the same stories over and over again. He pushed me to play whether I was hurt or not, insisting my injuries were no big deal. He fancies himself as some sort of debonair Frank Sinatra character, decorating the locker room with hundreds of photographs of people he claims to know. He seems angry all the time, as if he were chairman of the board of IBM and everybody around him were taking up his valuable time. He thinks he's the greatest card shark since Diamond Jim Brady. And he dresses like a guy who mistakenly thought double-knits were the cover of this month's *Gentleman's Quarterly*.

I guess I love him because he's Chop.

The best friend I had for the past nine years in Denver.

The guy who nursed my wounds and kept my creaky body intact during the rigorous campaigns of the NBA.

The guy who always stood beside me, whether I was in a shooting slump, road-weary from the long travels, or was just feeling sorry myself.

The guy who was my sidekick everywhere on the road, from

the coffee shops to the race tracks, there when I needed a friend.

Bob "Chopper" Travaglini, trainer for the Nuggets, was, and is, one of the special people in my life.

People probably wonder how an old man like Chopper and a young man like me could ever strike up a relationship. Sometimes I wondered that myself. I think it was because I always picked up the check. I'm worried about leaving Chopper behind, because I don't know how he's going to eat now that I'm gone.

I seriously considered writing Chop off as a dependent on last year's income taxes. The last time he picked up a check at a restaurant was when he thought he'd find a dollar bill underneath it. I think Roosevelt was president. Teddy.

Certainly I wouldn't want to create the impression that Chopper is stingy or cheap. He's very generous, as long as it doesn't involve his own money.

All kidding aside, if they ever have a Hall of Fame for trainers, Chopper deserves to be inducted. As long as there is no induction fee.

Chop's the best.

You've heard of a jack of all trades. Chopper is an ace of all trades. He can do anything. And what he can't do, he'll convince you he *could* do it if he wanted to.

He is a legend. He's more than a trainer. He's everything.

Chopper is part mother. He's there waiting with the Band-Aid when you come in with a skinned knee.

Chopper is part father. In addition to being the Nuggets' trainer, he's also the traveling secretary, so he's forever shepherding a group of aimless wanderers through airports.

Chopper is part priest. He hears everybody's problems and is always genuinely concerned, whether it's sitting up the night with rookie Willie White in the lobby of a Salt Lake City hotel trying to relax him so he'll play well in his first starting role the next day, or whether it's reassuring an aging veteran that his knee isn't that badly hurt and his career isn't really in jeopardy.

Chopper is part camp counselor. The butt of most of the team's jokes and pranks, sometimes he gets his feelings hurt. He likes being kidded by Doug and the players to a point, but sometimes it can be carried too far. I think it's ironic how the players tend to forget that he has feelings too.

Chop is truly one of the last Damon Runyon characters in sport. He is easily one of the NBA's most popular and well-known figures. Even referees come over to the Nugget bench during the game and say, "Chop, can you look at my ankle, I think it's sprained." Chop gets that even when he's the visiting trainer.

I hate to admit this, but now that I'm retired and won't have to put up with hearing him crow about it, I'll go ahead: I truly think Chopper was blessed with a divine gift of healing. I'm serious about that. He's amazing. He can diagnose an injury with the best; it's amazing how many times Chopper's diagnosis of the injury is confirmed by doctors. And the guy never had one whit of medical training. In fact, he never even had one whit of training as a trainer. He just knows because he knows. It's eerie.

Sometimes I wonder if the players and the Nugget management know what a jewel they've got in this guy. He has a rare understanding of the professional athlete, and nobody in the NBA gets players back in action faster than Chopper. Most of us are big babies when it comes to injuries and how our careers will be affected, and Chopper has the ability to get us through the physical aspect of the injury while also treating the mental aspect. So Chopper is probably equal parts trainer and psychologist, Chopper restores players' confidence so they can play with a little pain.

When the team is on the road, Chopper is the most important man in the franchise, responsible for a bunch of helpless athletes who have been spoon-fed all their lives. With the Nuggets, where the coaches don't often travel with the players, which makes Chop's role even more important. He takes care of boarding passes, gets the players seats on the plane, befriends the skycaps, and carries players' bags to the hotel. That may not sound like a big deal, but when you're moving that much stuff that often, there's a great margin for error. With Chopper, you don't have to worry about your bag being in your room, if you've got the right bag, or if your hotel reservation is made. Chop makes sure everything you need is there.

Maybe we on the team were spoiled by the Nuggets, for we took all that for granted. In my final days with the team, when Chopper was so helpful to me in making all my arrangements, my affection for him grew even greater. The day I left town, I drove by his place in my pickup truck—the one given to me by Red McCombs—to say goodbye. Chop was so choked up, he couldn't even say goodbye, so he just waved and walked away. When I drove off, I felt I was leaving part of me behind in Denver.

The first time I ever met Chopper was 1970 at the ABA All-Star Game in Greensboro. He was the trainer for the Eastern Division. This was my first chance to see a great trainer in action, because Chopper did everything from washing uniforms to giving the players pre-game massages.

Chopper was trainer for the Virginia Squires back then, and the hotel room he lived in was always the focal point of any social gathering among sports types, a country club for jocks. You didn't go to the coffee shop or the bar or the lobby; you went to Chopper's room. There was always a poker game or a crap game going on, and you could count on him having a cold beer for you. One night when the Colonels played the Squires, I went over to Chop's room after the Yankees had played the Mets in an exhibition game in Norfolk. I walked in and there was Ralph Kiner, the Mets' announcer and former Pirate great; Met third baseman Jim Fregosi; and Yankee pitching great Whitey Ford, all telling old-time baseball stories. I was absolutely transfixed.

Chopper's involvement with sports all started with the Penn's Grove (New Jersey) Raiders. He came out of the Air Force in the mid-fifties after serving in Korea and went to work at DuPont. One day while he was out riding, Chopper stopped to visit with a bunch of friends playing sandlot football and wound up as president, trainer, water boy, and chief bottle washer of the Penn's Grove Raiders. "I told them, 'You guys are doing this all wrong,' " says Chopper. "And they said, 'Okay, Chopper, you run it.' So I did."

The Penn's Grove Raiders lost the semi-pro championship by a point to the Swedesboro Devils, but the two teams wound up merging. A guy named Joe Vicere, the Devil quarterback, asked Chopper to tape his ankles one day. "So I started taping them, even though I'd never done it," says Chopper. "I didn't know shit about it."

When the Swedesboro Devils eventually folded, Chopper wound up working with Little League baseball and a couple of friends at his old high school, St. James.

One fateful day, Chopper was headed for the track but ran into a good friend of his, Joe Cacia, then athletic director at St. James, who talked him into riding down to Pearson's Sporting Goods in Philadelphia instead. "He conned me," says Chopper. As soon as Chopper met proprietor Jack Pearson, he asked: "You want a job with a pro team?"

Chopper started shaking all over, he was so scared. "I got sick, I wanted to throw up, I didn't know what to say," Chopper says. Shortly thereafter, he became trainer of the Philadelphia Bulldogs of the Continental Football League. He kept working hard, getting on-the-job training, and improving.

When the Continental Football League folded, Chopper bounced around with a few other minor-league teams. One day in 1968, Al Domenico, trainer of the Philadelphia 76ers, called to say that the Washington Capitals of the ABA were looking for a trainer. That would turn out to be Chopper. And that's where Chopper met up with a guy named Larry Brown, who would go on to coach the Denver Nuggets.

Chop likes to talk. He talks tough, like a guy from New Jersey, which he is, and is very brash. When I was a wide-eyed rookie, I was enamored of his stories. And did he have stories. Don't ever play "Can You Top Chop?" because any story you've got, he'll come up with some stuff that will curl your hair.

Being around Chopper for nearly a decade, I've heard all his stories four or five times each. At first I questioned their accuracy because Chopper embellished them a little more each time—he was known for never letting the facts get in the way of a good story. But even though the embellishment might vary, the story lines never changed. I told Chop that he ought to catalog the stories. Then, when somebody asks about Wayne Hardin and the Philadelphia Bulldogs, Chopper could just say "7B."

Chop didn't think that was funny.

Unfortunately, I never could get him to tell the exact story of how he got the nickname of "Chopper." All I know is that Rick Barry gave it to him when Chopper was the trainer in Washington. Something about Chop eating all the time on the airplane. When you ask Chop, he beats around the bush.

Sometimes Chopper talks a little too much and his credibility starts to sag. But just about the time you start doubting him, he pulls a rabbit out of the hat.

For instance, in fall 1984 my brother Greg called to ask me if I had any way of getting a couple of tickets to see the San Diego Padres–Chicago Cubs playoff game at Wrigley Field. Greg's wife, Paula, works at a bank in Batavia and the banks usually have most of the tickets, so if he couldn't get tickets, who could? I couldn't. Those were hot tickets, and it was impossible.

Just in passing, I mentioned this to Chopper. "I'll get him a couple," said Chopper. Very skeptical, I thought he'd gone too far on this one. "Sure," I said. He picked up the telephone and called Jack McKeon, general manager of the Padres.

"Jack," he said. "I need two tickets for Issel's brother to your game with the Cubs." The next day Greg went by McKeon's hotel room and found a pair of tickets awaiting him. Truly amazing!

Just when you start to doubt Chopper, he comes through.

The legend of Chopper grows annually. The most incredible tale about him I have heard was about the time when he ran out and flagged down a plane. I wasn't there, but Doug Moe swears it's true.

This was long before the age of security devices around airports; you just walked out the back door, and there were the runways. Chopper was running late getting the team to the airport and the plane had pulled away from the gate. It was sitting at the end of the runway, ready to take off. As the plane started to taxi, Chopper ran after it. He screamed and flapped his arms for the pilot to come back and pick up his players. He demanded that plane stop and return to the gate.

It did.

If nothing else, Chopper makes for a good target. Since the life of a pro basketball player is so boring, we entertained ourselves by kidding Chopper about his wardrobe or hairstyle or just generally made fun of him. And he was the butt of most of the Nugget players' pranks.

The Chopper Watchers on the team—like Glen "Gondo" Gondrezick, Bill Hanzlik, and I—had a rating system for his temper tantrums. In the first stage he just gets a little upset and starts swearing. In the second stage, he starts swearing a lot, raising his voice, and pacing. In the third stage, the vein in Chopper's forehead starts popping out.

Gondo was unmerciful, absolutely one of the nuttiest guys I've ever met. When we were at training camp in Alamosa, Colorado, a few years ago, Glen, Dave Robisch, and I would get each other's room keys and trash each other's places—remove all the light bulbs, turn the beds upside down, drag the mattress out to the parking lot. Admittedly these were juvenile stunts right out of junior high school summer camp, but we were bored and it broke the monotony.

Gondo decided it would be fun to trash Chopper's room. When Chopper got back to his room and saw his clothes all over, his mattress in the parking lot, and all the light bulbs removed, he went absolutely nuts, reaching the *fifth* stage that night. We should have known a guy like Chop, nearly 50 years old, would fail to see the humor in our childish prank. We just didn't know how *much* he would fail to see it.

I'd seen Chopper reach fifth stage only once before, as a result of the best prank we ever pulled on him, the time we were snowbound in the Marriott Hotel at Chicago's O'Hare Airport. We played in Detroit on December 23, 1982, and a huge snowstorm hit Denver the next day. Stapleton Field in Denver was closed, and we couldn't get back for Christmas. It was the pits.

I had flown to Lexington from Detroit and was lucky enough to be with my family. I was supposed to take the family back to Denver from Lexington on Christmas morning, but the flight from Lexington to Denver was canceled. So I called Denver and found out the Nuggets had made it from Detroit to Chicago. Knowing Chopper, I figured that if anybody would be on that first flight out of Chicago to Denver, it would be the Nuggets—even if he had to run out and flag down another plane.

So the Issel family took the next flight out of Lexington to Chicago and met the team there. We weren't going anywhere, but at least I was there with my family, which was more than my teammates could say.

It was chaotic: Chopper was in his element. He set up "Snow Central" in the lobby of the hotel and was on the phone every minute. Naturally, he had the home telephone number of the supervisor of United Airlines, with whom he was on a first-name basis. He was in total command, and to Chopper that's power.

But even Chopper was powerless in the situation; every time he called, the airline told him it would be three days before we could get out. Of course, the players were really riding him about his lack of influence. Suddenly there was a call on Chopper's hotline from a guy who said he was a supervisor from United. "There will be a plane ready for you in an hour, Mr. Travaglini," the man said. Chopper's chest puffed up with pride as he announced it to everyone in the lobby, rounded up the players—we all knew what was going down—and stacked up all the equipment in the lobby. He was crowing to everyone, "We're going in an hour!" as if he had pulled off a miracle.

You can imagine Chopper's outrage when he discovered that he'd been had—that it had been Glen Godrezick on the phone, not a United supervisor. We didn't get out of Chicago until the day after Christmas. Gondo wound up getting cut from the team the next year.

I always wondered if Chopper had a vote.

It's extremely difficult for a pro athlete to make a friend and keep that friend throughout his career. There are too many pressures on those friendships.

Chopper was an unlikely friend. I'll bet there aren't another NBA player and trainer as close as we've been for nine years. One day, maybe I'll name a horse after him. I'll call it "Free Lunch."

Professional athletes are so insecure and superstitious. They constantly worry about their careers coming to an abrupt halt due to injury, being traded, or having a new coach take over and say it's over. People have the attitude that if they get too close to a guy whose career is going the wrong way, it might be contagious, like the black plague.

And then there's the mental anguish of losing a friend. I guess it must be the same principle for soldiers in combat who become loners because they can't stand the sight of a friend lying there with a bullet in his skull. I know it sounds peculiar and egocentric, but it's the truth. Every time a friend ships out, he takes a piece of you with him, so you put it in your head that it's "better him than me." Early on, you learn to steel yourself against getting close to teammates—because one day you look around and they're gone. You live with a dozen guys for a season, some of them several seasons. Then, one day, without explanation, one of them is gone. Sometimes he doesn't even say goodbye; he just disappears into the night. We all hate that side of pro sports.

It's probably cruel, but we used to go through a morbid routine in the Nugget locker room when we found out somebody had been traded or cut: we would sing that old song, "Has Anybody Here Seen My Old Friend John?," changing the name to Fred or Tom or Bob. I'm sure that by the fall of 1985, somebody will have sung the song and inserted the name "Dan." In a way, I guess, that's a tribute. That was our way of dealing with the grief of losing a teammate—and that's exactly what it was, grief, for it is almost as if the departed player died.

In spite of all the pressures on friendships, I did make a couple of good friends on the teams I played for. One was

Louie Dampier, who I met at the University of Kentucky and later played with on the Colonels. We were close from the first day we met. Louie was a senior when I was a freshman, and since freshmen weren't allowed to have cars Louie would lend me his. He had a good sense of humor and, like me, always kept things in perspective by being just a tiny bit irreverent. You have to laugh at things, even at yourself. Otherwise, they come and take you away to the funny farm.

Louie and I were roommates for four years when we played with the Colonels. When I left the Colonels and went to Denver, we went on to San Antonio for a few years, but we still stayed in touch—which is very unusual for pro ball. Louie and I remain good friends, and I still see him occasionally.

Of friends I've met in basketball, Kim Hughes is one of my best although we played together only two seasons. He lived in Denver, and I saw a lot of him when he wasn't playing in Italy.

It's funny how close our careers have paralleled. He went to the University of Wisconsin, as I very nearly did. We're both centers. We both started in the ABA. Kim played with the Nuggets during the 1978–79 and 1980–81 seasons but had far greater success in Italy.

He's one of the premier players in the Italian League, and he'd have to take a big cut to leave there, but I think he would be a hell of a pickup for Denver, and the Nuggets did talk to him during the summer of 1985. He would be an excellent backup center, although he's primarily a defensive player. Guys who are 6'11" and can really play are rare commodities. And I think he's gotten a bum rap on his scoring; he's a lot better shooter than he's given credit for being.

I consider many players friends just from knowing them as opponents—like Kareem—but very few were close pals. I've made other friends on the Colonels and the Nuggets, but players see so much of their teammates at work that they want to get away from each other's personal lives. It's difficult to maintain friendships with people outside of basketball because they have totally different schedules; as a player, your Tuesday night is pretty much the same as your Saturday night during the season. You can't go bowling with your neighbors. You can't have a weekend foursome for golf. You don't even have time for the PTA meetings or your son's ball game or your daughter's play.

Don't get me wrong, I'm not really complaining. Basketball gave the Issels a very, very good life. But, contrary to popular opinion, pro basketball players don't spend every night hanging around local night spots like the Colorado Mining Company or the Denver Denver. It's a fairly routine social life.

Another one of my best friends turned out to be a guy in the media, Ron Zappolo of KCNC-TV. That's always risky, both for the player and for the media person, because it's difficult to separate business and friendship. To Ron's credit, he was always able to do that and, hopefully, it never compromised his position. I always felt I could trust Ron, but I also knew he had a job to do. And if one night I stunk up the joint—missed a shot that would have won the game, or whatever—I knew Ron wasn't going to be able to ignore that. He treated me fairly, and I tried to be considerate of other TV reporters without showing partiality toward him.

Although, now that I'm gone, I'm sure Ron's ratings will start to slip.

Roommates make good short-term friends. You can share a lot during that period of time. I've had some good roommates and some weird ones.

My first roommate at the University of Kentucky was Mike Pratt, and we lasted only about two months. I guess we were too much alike, because we just couldn't get along. So, by mutual consent, we changed. He moved in with Mike Casey and I roomed with Randy Pool.

That proved to be a bigger mistake. Pool was the biggest slob I ever met. He would have two week's worth of clothes piled on top of his chair and newspapers all over the floor. I made it through my freshman year, and then I switched again.

My sophomore year at Kentucky, I roomed with Mike Casey. That was enjoyable. We had a good time socially, and both of us had successful years on the court.

My junior year, I roomed with Greg Sterrick, the guy who was getting beaten down by the coaching staff and eventually left school. Those were tough times for Greg and not very good ones for me. I probably could have been a lot more help to Greg, but by that time I hated being in the dorm. I was dating Cheri by then, and every chance I got I was over at her parents' house. I would get back to the dorm just in time to meet curfew every night.

My senior year, I was married and got a permanent roommate, the best one I ever had.

On the road with the Colonels my rookie year, I roomed with Darrell Carrier from the University of Western Kentucky. He was an interesting guy, having come up the hard way by playing in the industrial leagues, so he had some stories. Despite the terrible conditions of the ABA, flying puddle-jumper airplanes to small cities, those were fun days. Louie Dampier and I had many good times together.

Once I got to Denver, I roomed on the road with my "twin," Byron Beck, a local boy who had played for the University of Denver. People thought we looked alike, since we were both blonde and about the same size. One day I was at the Water Board in downtown Denver getting a permit to water my lawn, and this guy kept saying, "I know you're Byron Beck." And I kept saying, "No, I'm not!" He thought I was lying to him. Of course, Byron wasn't a bad guy to be mistaken for, because he was well thought of in Denver. Having him for a roommate and friend helped me make an easy transition from Louisville to Denver.

Then I roomed with Kim Hughes, then Mack Calvin, a great player with the Nuggets. About that time, the NBA started giving each player his own room on the road, and I never liked it as much. Having company after a bad night, or even a good night, was an excellent way to kill an evening. Even the bad roommates were good to have around. Otherwise, it was just terminal boredom.

Another Denver friendship that I really value is that of Paula Hansen, the former Nugget vice-president and assistant general manager, who left to join the New York NBA office in mid-1985. Not many people outside the Nuggets knew much about her, but to me she was the most important cog in the front office.

Until she left, Paula was the only person who had logged more service with the Nuggets than I had. She did a lot of the thankless jobs that have to be done if an organization is to be successful, but she never got the credit. She made the contacts in the community. When a new player came to town and needed a place to live, Paula would call the real estate people. If you needed to buy a washing machine or car or just get tickets to the circus for your kids, Paula was always there and willing to help. Paula Hansen did more for me than any person in the city of Denver in the 10 years I was there. Of course, she never taped my ankles or went to the racetrack with me, but Paula was a great friend without whom I couldn't have functioned.

The best compliment I can pay her is that if I owned an NBA team, I can't think of a better person to run it than Paula Hansen. I know she'll be great in the New York NBA office and I wish her the best.

Friends are priceless, and I'm certainly going to miss the ones I've left behind in Denver. But I've got new things waiting for me now. For the first time since I was in the eighth grade, there will be no basketball for Dan Issel. Right now, I feel no pangs, and I look forward wholeheartedly to life down on the farm.

I know this is going to be a lonely situation at times. There is no cheering crowd; horses aren't going to give me a standing ovation every morning when I come down to the barn. But I doubt if I'll ever miss the cheering crowds again.

Unless, of course, I'm standing in the winner's circle on Derby Day. That I could handle.

14
LOOKING BACKWARD AT LIFE FROM DOWN ON THE KENTUCKY FARM

It was raining in Versailles (pronounced Ver-SALES), Kentucky, as Dan Issel climbed into a golf cart and negotiated a gravel road on the way to a grassy knoll. From there, you could see the clusters of oaks punctuating the green rolling hills of Courtland Farm, which ambles over 160 acres, hard against Huntertown Road. It is home now to Dan Issel, whose nickname, ironically, has been "the Horse" for more than a decade. There, from his favorite vantage point on the farm, with rain pitter-pattering on the roof of the cart, Issel talked about the new life ahead and the old one he was leaving behind.

Some of us are just 'fraidy cats who are motivated by negative influences in our lives. I've already admitted that I was driven by fear of failure, right down to the day I retired. Tucked away somewhere in the dark recesses of my mind was that picture of Willie Mays in the 1973 World Series, chasing fly balls and falling down because his legs were too old. His heart wanted to do it, but his body just couldn't go anymore. What a nightmare for him, and for all of us who can remember him when he ran forever in centerfield.

I hoped that would never happen to me and I was going to do everything in my power to avoid it.

With today's generous salaries, there is no need for a veteran pro athlete to wind up on welfare. Above all else, I didn't want to find myself in the lobby of Caesar's Palace someday, shaking hands with the customers and saying, "Hi, I'm Dan Issel. Remember me from 20 years ago? I played pro basketball. Want to hear some stories?"

Hopefully, people will remember I played a little basketball. But I don't want that to be the only thing I ever accomplished in my life.

I'm proud of this farm and I'm proud of how I was able to achieve getting here. Yet I'm not foolish enough to think that if I had been 6'1", I would have been able to do it. I think I would have been successful at something, but it probably wouldn't have been basketball.

I think I was able to accomplish whatever I accomplished through hard work and not necessarily through God-given ability. I'm thankful for the tools the good Lord gave me. True, I was blessed with a 6'9" body, but I was never able to jump very high or run very fast—anybody who ever saw me play never confused me with Dr. J. But a lot of players with a great deal more talent than I had weren't able to give the effort it takes to compete, for whatever reason.

I don't like to sound like a martyr, but I believe in the John Houseman school of finance when it comes to sports: you should *earn* your way.

That's what it takes to be all you can be in life. I learned that from my high school coach, Coach Vandersnick, and from Coach Rupp. They came from the old school: if you were going to attempt something, you might as well put 110 percent into it.

Coach Rupp told me something a long time ago that I never forgot: if you accomplish something, a lot of people will come up to you and say, "Gosh, that's nice, you sure were lucky to accomplish that." Coach Rupp always said the harder you worked, the luckier you seemed to get.

People tell me I'm lucky to be retiring. And I tell them I was retired for 15 years, and now the real work begins in the real world. I'm going to be so busy on this farm that I won't miss basketball. As the autumn approaches, I'm looking forward to seeing football games at the University of Kentucky, not having to do all that painful running to get into peak condition, and not having to face another long season of travel. This is what I've worked for, what I've dreamed about for the last five or six years while I was sitting alone in all those lonely hotel rooms.

So this is a great feeling of accomplishment for me. Basketball was a lot of fun, but it was a means to an end. This is that end. I never expected it to last forever. When I signed with the Colonels, Cheri and I thought it might last five years. Instead it lasted 15. I can honestly say that for 15 years I gave everything I had to give on the court. That was my upbringing—middle class, rural America—and it was ground into me since I was a kid: to play as hard as I could.

I don't want it to sound like every night was terrific and I was great. There were lots of nights that I stunk. Those nights hurt. But people are more forgiving if they think you're out there trying hard. Then they make concessions for your flaws.

The worst thing you can do is look back and say, "I could have accomplished this or that if only I would have tried harder." So far, I'm not in that position. With this new life, I don't think I'm going to be in it either. You're pretty responsible for the things that happen to you. And I plan to run this farm the same way I played the game of basketball: with 110 percent effort.

I'm sure that on some days I'll stink. But that will be because I was down at the barns, shoveling horse manure.

Spending part of my youth on the farm in Missouri, I discovered at an early age that there was a certain serenity and solitude about it that I enjoyed. It was there that I first developed my love for animals, but it wasn't until later that I discovered horses. I was a college sophomore when my current partner, Tom Gentry, took Cheri and me to the races at Keeneland. We didn't have very much money in college and that night we won $65 betting. That seemed like all the money in the world.

I don't think Gentry gave us another winner the rest of the

time we were in college, but I was hooked. I fell in love with horses. And not just because of the wagering, although I doubt I would go to the track if I couldn't bet a bob or two. For that matter, there wouldn't be racetracks if you couldn't bet.

The things I enjoy about racing are the same things that are important to me in other areas of my life. Tradition. You go to the Kentucky Derby and you realize that this is the biggest race in the world for three-year-olds and it's been going on now for 110 years. It's amazing how much the lives of the owner and the trainer and everybody connected with the horse can be changed by that one race. And the horse goes down in immortality.

My first Derby was probably the most unusual one in the history of the race. Cheri and I watched the race from the infield in 1968, the year that Dancer's Image won the race but was disqualified when tests revealed he had phenylbutazone, a pain-killing drug, in his blood. All the bets on Dancer's Image were paid off, but the race and the purse went to Forward Pass, the second-place horse.

Actually, I was in the infield and I hardly saw a horse all day because it's difficult to see from there. Still, I experienced the rush of the moment. I can still remember having goosebumps when they said, "Ladies and Gentlemen, the Kentucky Derby!" and then played "My Old Kentucky Home." I still get goosebumps.

In 1968 it was like being at a picnic, not a horse race, but the following year I saw my first Derby from the stands. Gentry got us good seats and we actually saw Bill Hartack ride Majestic Prince for the win. I've tried to make them all since then, but sometimes the basketball season prevented me from going.

One Derby that I missed—and missed in more ways than one—was Secretariat's win in 1973. The Colonels were playing the Indiana Pacers in one of the few nationally televised ABA games. The announcers knew I was a big fan of horse racing, so they asked me before the game who I picked to win. I made the biggest fool of myself—even bigger than I ever made playing basketball—when they asked for my prediction: I picked Sham to win the Derby. Sham was a horse with great heart, but

Secretariat was on his way to winning the first triple crown in 25 years and breaking Sham's heart that day, as well as mine. So I have the distinction of going on national TV and picking against the greatest racehorse of all time.

I hope to make all the triple crown races now, but I've only been to the Preakness once and the Belmont a few times. I was at Belmont Park to see Steve Cauthen ride Affirmed to his triple-crown win over Alydar in what I consider the greatest race ever run. Alydar hooked him at the head of the stretch and they raced as a team all the way through the stretch. Affirmed just would not let Alydar get by him. It was chilling.

That was a great moment. And I was also at Belmont for the saddest occasion in racing I've ever witnessed—the day when Foolish Pleasure and Ruffian were running a match race. But Ruffian was just unbeatable. When she was racing against her own class and her own sex, there were no fillies that could even warm her up. But Ruffian broke down and had to be destroyed. Whether or not Foolish Pleasure would have beaten her that day is open to debate.

Some horses just capture the public's imagination. Another horse like that was Canonera II. A lot of people don't realize that Canonero II was a Kentucky-bred horse, because he raced in Puerto Rico and developed a great Hispanic following.

Still, Secretariat is the greatest horse I've ever seen set foot on a track—even though I didn't pick him to win the Kentucky Derby that year. Some people knock Secretariat for not yet reproducing himself in stud. But it might be a long time before we ever see another Secretariat.

Like never.

The Derby is the glamour race, but I also enjoy going to Keeneland in Lexington and watching racing in its purest form. The motto at Keeneland is "Racing as It Was Meant to Be." There isn't even a track announcer. They bring the horses out on the track with the bugle. They warm them up. They put them in the gate. And they run them. If you're not paying attention, you'll miss the race entirely.

It's then that you realize that men built this track more than 100 years ago. I love that tradition.

Most of all, I love the horses, no matter what track they're racing on. Some people may have thought I resented the nickname "the Horse," but I didn't. I think the nickname is neat. It was given to me by Bob King, who was assistant general manager of the Nuggets when I started playing for them. Bob went from the Nuggets to the New York NBA office and is now back working for Carl Scheer of the Clippers. He's a horse freak just like I am. Bob was always a part of our little group, who, along with Chopper, would take in the races at Centennial in Denver before they finally tore it down.

Bob said he gave me the name because I played like a horse. Not like a thoroughbred, like a Clydesdale.

All kidding aside, I can see a parallel between our lives and those of horses. When a baby first stands up on its wobbly legs, it's a beautiful thing to see the mother nurture it. Just like humans, horses have setbacks—sicknesses and deformities, crooked limbs. But that baby still has a chance to grow up someday and stand in the winner's circle.

The prettiest time is the spring, when the foals are brand new. They are out exploring, lumbering through the grass, and they begin to wander farther and farther away from their mothers, getting bolder and bolder. They never completely take their eye off her; they know exactly where she is and what she's doing at all times. They are growing up, just like we did.

The spring is so joyous, because the earth is reborn with new leaves and new blossoms, and we all have new hope—hope all over again that one of those little fellas or gals with the spindly legs could turn out some day to be a Kentucky Derby winner.

A horse can have great bloodlines, yet it might not be able to outrun you and me simply because it doesn't have the heart to compete. You see a horse like John Henry, the greatest money winner of all time in thoroughbred racing. He sold for only $1,100 and they thought so little of his bloodlines that he was castrated as a young horse. He refuses to get beat and he goes on and on and on. At the first Arlington Million at Arlington Park in Chicago, John Henry was ahead by a nose. In fact, the

TV announcer called a horse named the Bart the winner of the race, but John Henry stuck his nose in front, and he won the photo finish. You'll never convince me that John Henry doesn't have the heart of a winner.

I've seen that so many times in my basketball career: people who didn't have the ability, but were great because they put everything they had into the game. And I saw players who had a world of physical ability but still were never successful because they didn't have the heart.

I guess what I love so much about the horse business is the rural setting and the peaceful atmosphere. Yet I'm involved in a very competitive sport with beautiful athletes—yes, athletes. And there is a very big similarity between equine athletes and human athletes. Except that horses don't miss airplanes, skip practices, or talk back to their bosses.

Admittedly, I probably took some of my life as a basketball player for granted. When the cheering stops, only then do you begin to really appreciate what it used to sound like. On the other hand, there were always a lot of responsibilities that went along with the cheers. I had to share my life with an awful lot of people, and that wasn't always fun.

I know this is going to be a much lonelier situation at times, even more so than staying in hotel rooms by myself. There is no cheering crowd; horses aren't going to give me a standing ovation every morning when I come down to the barn. My teammates are fewer—Cheri and my farm manager, Jody Alexander. But when the day's work is over, I can come home to my family and do the things that are important to me. Playing basketball before 17,000 people was exciting, but I'm excited about this life, too. I doubt if I'll ever want or miss the cheering crowds or the spotlight again.

Unless, of course, someday I'm standing in the winner's circle at Churchill Downs on Derby Day. That I could handle.

I'm proud of the way I conducted myself during my basketball career. I can't say that I'm proud of every moment I was on the court, because I made some mistakes. Hopefully, though, I can hold my head up high as I leave the game. I'm proud of whatever respect I might have earned—expecially because I wanted to be an example for my children. I pray that Sheridan and Scott will want to conduct their lives in a similar way, not taking the shortcuts, but putting forth a supreme effort at whatever they tackle.

Sheridan is already showing signs of it in her schoolwork. It doesn't come easily for her, but she sits right there and hammers at it until she gets it. I'm especially proud that she was a straight A student at a very tough Denver school. At the age of 13, she'd already studied four years of French. She also learned a great deal of responsibility riding and caring for her horse. She was required to do all the chores that come with the daily grooming. And showing the horse in competition, she must go into the ring and learn to win and lose. That gave her a great deal of maturity early.

I want both my children to put their hearts into whatever they attempt, and it doesn't have to be sports.

Things come easier for Scott and it took him a while to develop the same kind of drive to succeed that Sheridan has. It really began to surface when he joined a youth soccer league in the fall of 1985. His team, the Rowdies, was unbeaten and unscored upon through September. And Scott was one of the goalies. He was thrilled to see his name in print. Like father, like son.

Scott is a big sports fan. He knows all the names of the players in basketball and all the scoring averages of the Nuggets. But he saw his dad as somebody who just hung around the team; he didn't see me in the same context as Kiki or Alex or Calvin.

Maybe I'm wrong, though, because you never know what a child's eyes can see. And, besides, Scott is on record to the contrary. When Scott was just three, Irv Moss of *The Post* did an interview with him, one of those question-and-answer deals, except that Irv did it more like Art Linkletter would have. It went something like this:

QUESTION: Who is your favorite player?

SCOTT: Cedrick [Hordges] and Gondo [Glen Gondrezick]. They're not the best.

QUESTION: What number does David Thompson wear?

SCOTT: Three three

QUESTION: What happened to Dave Robisch?

SCOTT: He sparkled his knee and he broke this part [pointing to his heel].

QUESTION: Who's the fattest Nugget?

SCOTT: Chopper [Bob Travaglini]. He doesn't play. He's the trainer.

QUESTION: Who's number 44?

SCOTT: My dad. He's really a good player.

Maybe the brainwashing worked after all.

So it has all come down to this: the farm, my family and friends, my horses, and a few memories.

I can hardly express the feeling of peace and gratitude that overcome me when I am out on this hill, looking over the land. It is a feeling of oneness with the universe, a feeling I never was able to attain as an athlete. This must have been the way kings felt when they surveyed their kingdoms. Except I'm not gloating; I am humbled by its spectacular beauty.

My life has been one big storybook and the good Lord has been generous with his blessings. I am overjoyed, being here with Cheri and watching Sheridan grow into a young woman and Scott become a young man. This will be my first year as a full-time father.

And I am pleased to feel that I have nothing more to prove as a basketball player, although some people don't believe that. Doug Moe always says that as soon as basketball season rolls around and Cheri starts asking me to do chores around the house, I'll be calling him and begging to come back. Don't wait up or leave a light burning in your window, Doug. No chance.

That's just because Doug has been around a basketball for so long that he's beginning to think like one.

My hopes and dreams are here now. This may very well be my final resting place. Yes, maybe there under that tree. An epitaph? Something simple would do, like, "Here lies Dan Issel, father, husband, and horseman. He always tried hard and gave his best." Something like that.

Maybe you could add one line about basketball. Such as, "without whom Doug Moe would never have been the legend he is today."

As I close my eyes and look back on my basketball career, I don't see anything, like a game or a shot or an incident, in a single freeze frame. I tend to think of whole experiences.

My mind goes back to 1975, when the Colonels won the ABA championship. That was the only one of my career, and it becomes more precious as the years fly by. You hear athletes talk a lot about winning championships, as if they had some kind of religious experience. And sometimes you wonder about the sincerity of those statements. It was a very important chapter in my life, and I shall always treasure that achievement.

This isn't false modesty, but very few of the individual plateaus I reached during 15 seasons really seemed significant. Oh, indeed, I would have liked more recognition and more championships. You have to be motivated by something, and fame is certainly an appealing lure to most of us. Oddly enough, I am the least famous person on pro basketball's list of top ten all-time scorers. You have to be fairly obscure to be number four on the list and still not be very well known outside Denver and Kentucky.

There was one night, though, that meant a great deal to me. It was the very first game of my 14th season, the home opener against Utah. I needed eight points that night to reach a total of 25,000. Something struck me about looking down that list of nine or ten names and seeing the select company I would join—Kareem, Wilt, Oscar, Julius, West, etc.

The funniest part about that night is that the Nuggets had given out posters of me and planned a halftime ceremony around reaching the 25,000-point plateau. Talk about pressure! That kind of thing can be scary: I remember a few years ago a running back for the Atlanta Falcons reached 1,000 yards for the season in the last game. They called time out, presented him with the football, he went back into the game, carried the ball, and lost yardage. He wound up under the mark for the season. An incident like that can be humiliating.

Being the Nervous Nellie that I am, I went out and scored my eight points as soon as I could. And later I told the press, "That ceremony could have been awfully dull if I hadn't made the eight points." They asked me if I'd worried about failing to make the eight points, which shows you how much the media thought of my shooting toward the end. And I said that I was totally confident, "because Scott told me this morning I could do it."

It was a fun time, a pleasant time, and it is even more gratifying to me now than it was. Moe probably paid me the supreme compliment when he told the media, "If you locked me in a gym for 15 years, I still couldn't score 25,000 points."

You tend to live in a fantasy world when you are an athlete, and it's not always easy to gauge your accomplishments. Your previous life is sometimes best told in yellowing newspaper headlines, some good, some bad.

"Issel Feels Heat, Asks Brown Not To Play Him" was one of those bad ones, and it conjures up the image of my struggles with Larry Brown. But you have to take the bitter with the sweet.

Another one was "Issel Doesn't Find Camaraderie There Was In Old ABA." That was in 1979, and you could tell I was still a little homesick for both Kentucky and the old ABA. I wasn't complaining; I was just trying to be honest in response to a reporter's question.

And it's true that we all had deeper feelings for each other in the ABA, maybe because we were in the mess together. With so much instability, we never knew for sure if the checks were going to stop coming or if the franchise would be out of business the next week. And yet those were such happy times. Artis Gilmore and I were friends and he was such a force on the court. We had a bunch of scorers, so we could gamble on defense and Artis could cover our mistakes. (I found out just how much of a force he was when I was traded and wound up having to play against him at center.)

"Horse Isn't Ready For Pasture" in 1980 reminds me of my negotiations with the Nuggets. Those times are not very pleasant for an athlete. I wish there was a way to avoid it, but these days it appears everybody's looking for leverage. My only way was threatening to retire, although I never really wanted to go through with it back then. Luckily, there were five more seasons.

"Post-Career Challenges Lure Issel" in the 1983 *Denver Post* tells you I was thinking about the end even then. Actually, I'd been thinking about it three years prior. And "Counting Minutes: Issel Adjusting To Aches Of Age" from 1984 tells you my body was getting ready, too.

None of the headlines strike such horror into my heart, though, as "Issel sold to Baltimore Claws." If I could, I'd rewrite that one out of my life, even though it taught me some valuable lessons about the mercenary aspects of sports. It is as vivid as yesterday: practicing those days with the Claws . . . John Y. Brown showing up at the hotel to cut a deal with me—getting him off the hook with the fans and press in Louisville and getting me out of Baltimore.

But the bad times were few.

That last chapter of headlines:

- "Teary Salute," the story of the Cancer Society's dinner honoring me and my family. I wanted Cheri and the kids with me. They were a comfort.
- "*Post* To Present Annual Dan Issel Award," which was very flattering and maybe will help them remember who I was in Denver by 1990. The Dan Issel Award goes annually to the athlete or private citizen who best exemplifies the spirit of community leadership in sports.
- "Nuggets Near Title With 118–109 Victory." As we beat San

Antonio on "Dan Issel Night" and moved closer to the Midwest Division title, it was such a great feeling.

- "Division Crown Pleasant Surprise For Retiring Dan Issel," the day after we beat Golden State, 130–125. Now we were starting to think about winning the Western Conference. And I kept preaching, "Anything is possible," hoping that we might mesmerize ourselves into beating the Lakers. It was a helluva ride in my final season and I will always be grateful for the efforts of my teammates who so badly wanted to win it all.

- And finally, "Last Hurrah! Three-Point Bomb Issel's Final Blast," the story of my last game in Los Angeles.

A tremendous feeling of relief overcame me that night in the Forum. Every time I ever ran out on the floor in my career, I gave it all I had—there was no other choice. Now, as that final basket came screaming down out of the California night and found its mark, the curtain was coming down with it.

I knew I would never again have to awaken the next morning and read the newspaper or listen to the radio while my performance from the night before was being critiqued publicly. I might be working just as hard, or harder, here on the farm, but my mistakes and my achievements will only be graded privately. That is a great comfort, as it was when I saw that last three-pointer explode into the net.

For me, it was the perfect Parting Shot.

the coffee shops to the race tracks, there when I needed a friend.

Bob "Chopper" Travaglini, trainer for the Nuggets, was, and is, one of the special people in my life.

People probably wonder how an old man like Chopper and a young man like me could ever strike up a relationship. Sometimes I wondered that myself. I think it was because I always picked up the check. I'm worried about leaving Chopper behind, because I don't know how he's going to eat now that I'm gone.

I seriously considered writing Chop off as a dependent on last year's income taxes. The last time he picked up a check at a restaurant was when he thought he'd find a dollar bill underneath it. I think Roosevelt was president. Teddy.

Certainly I wouldn't want to create the impression that Chopper is stingy or cheap. He's very generous, as long as it doesn't involve his own money.

All kidding aside, if they ever have a Hall of Fame for trainers, Chopper deserves to be inducted. As long as there is no induction fee.

Chop's the best.

You've heard of a jack of all trades. Chopper is an ace of all trades. He can do anything. And what he can't do, he'll convince you he *could* do it if he wanted to.

He is a legend. He's more than a trainer. He's everything.

Chopper is part mother. He's there waiting with the Band-Aid when you come in with a skinned knee.

Chopper is part father. In addition to being the Nuggets' trainer, he's also the traveling secretary, so he's forever shepherding a group of aimless wanderers through airports.

Chopper is part priest. He hears everybody's problems and is always genuinely concerned, whether it's sitting up the night with rookie Willie White in the lobby of a Salt Lake City hotel trying to relax him so he'll play well in his first starting role the next day, or whether it's reassuring an aging veteran that his knee isn't that badly hurt and his career isn't really in jeopardy.

Chopper is part camp counselor. The butt of most of the team's jokes and pranks, sometimes he gets his feelings hurt. He likes being kidded by Doug and the players to a point, but

13
MY PAL CHOPPER
AND OTHER FRIENDS LEFT
BEHIND IN THE ROCKIES

I don't know why I love Chopper like I do. He's gruff. He's full of hot air. He never picks up the check. He's always telling me the same stories over and over again. He pushed me to play whether I was hurt or not, insisting my injuries were no big deal. He fancies himself as some sort of debonair Frank Sinatra character, decorating the locker room with hundreds of photographs of people he claims to know. He seems angry all the time, as if he were chairman of the board of IBM and everybody around him were taking up his valuable time. He thinks he's the greatest card shark since Diamond Jim Brady. And he dresses like a guy who mistakenly thought double-knits were the cover of this month's *Gentleman's Quarterly*.

I guess I love him because he's Chop.

The best friend I had for the past nine years in Denver.

The guy who nursed my wounds and kept my creaky body intact during the rigorous campaigns of the NBA.

The guy who always stood beside me, whether I was in a shooting slump, road-weary from the long travels, or was just feeling sorry myself.

The guy who was my sidekick everywhere on the road, from